consent.

consent.

THE NEW RULES OF SEX EDUCATION

every teen's guide to
healthy sexual relationships

Jennifer Lang, MD

ALTHEA
PRESS

This book is dedicated to my teenage self.

And to Sheila, Nico, and Sofia. May you emerge into your bodies and lives with all the joy and self-love that you are entitled to by birthright.

CONTENTS

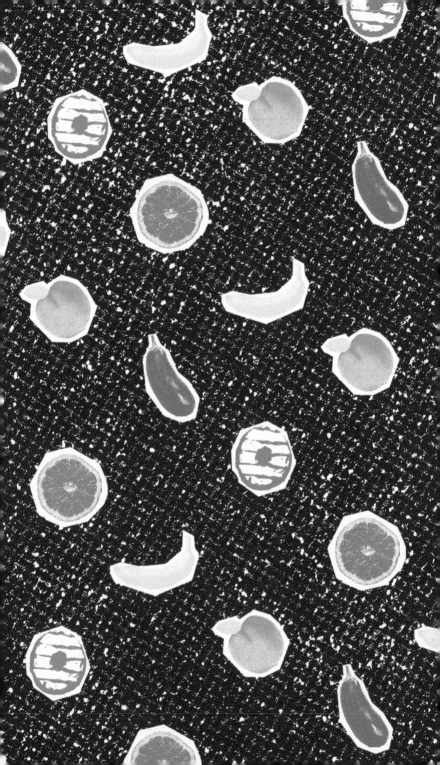

INTRODUCTION

So often sex education, or "sex ed," is presented as a laundry list of all the bad and scary things associated with sex. It's framed more as a cautionary tale than as a comprehensive education including all the pleasurable and fun parts of sex along with the potential dangers. Many states don't legally require sex ed to be medically accurate; many don't require schools to provide any information about sex at all.

Some parents and teachers may prefer the fear-based curriculums currently being taught in schools across the United States, but it doesn't appear to work for teens and young adults. Abstinence-based sex education—that is, sex education that teaches students they should never have sex before marriage—has been proven ineffective in study after study. Teens in abstinence-only programs are actually *more* likely to become pregnant or get sexually transmitted infections (STIs) than those whose education on the subject has been more comprehensive. When sex (or even talking about sex) is stigmatized, controlled, forbidden, or otherwise made taboo, the result is not that teens don't have sex—it's simply that they have sex without being prepared for it.

I'm a doctor, specifically a gynecologist, who has traveled the world talking to people about sexual and reproductive health. I'm also a parent who tries to respond to every sex-related question my kids have with a scientifically accurate, age-appropriate answer. Finally, I'm someone who believes that healthy sexuality can be a critical part of a healthy life and a healthy world.

Instead of making sexuality a forbidden topic, I believe we as a society need to talk about it openly, with the goal being *sexual literacy*. Of course we need to discuss risks, but we also need to discuss how to communicate with each other for mutual pleasure and enjoyment, how sexuality is highly individual and can change dramatically throughout one's lifetime, and how some people are very active in their sexual self-expression while others might find that no expression at all feels best. All of these choices can be healthy and normal, as long as no one is being hurt and everyone involved is giving consent.

Consent is perhaps the single most important thing to learn about in sex ed, and it will be emphasized throughout this book. Whether you identify as male, female, nonbinary, or something else, getting **ACTIVE, ENTHUSIASTIC CONSENT** from your partner is just about the only thing in sex that is an absolute *must* in every encounter. Every. Single. Time. And in order for that to happen, **YOU AND YOUR PARTNER BOTH NEED TO HAVE THE CAPACITY TO GIVE CONSENT.** Anyone involved in a sexual situation must be old enough, not overly intoxicated by alcohol or drugs, and not coerced into sex due to a power imbalance in the relationship. These can be tricky concepts, but don't worry—this book will break them down in a factual, understandable way.

Overall, this should be a clear, concise guidebook. You can read it cover to cover or skip around according to your interest. I'll be your guide on this journey, but I don't always have all the answers. If you want to know more about a particular subject, check out the Resources provided on page 103. I feel passionately that if people receive good information about sex, they are more likely to make smart and sensitive decisions, and I hope the information in this book empowers you to do just that.

WHAT'S IN THIS BOOK?

It wouldn't be possible to have a complete discussion of every aspect of human sexuality in a book of this size. Here's what this book will cover and what it won't.

THIS BOOK IS ABOUT:

INCLUSIVITY. No gender identity, sexual orientation, or amount of sexual expression is superior or inferior to any other.

FLUIDITY. Human beings grow and evolve throughout their lifetimes. Labels can be a great way to help someone understand or relate to another person's experience, but it's important to recognize that they don't fully define a person and they often change over time.

EMPATHY. Partnered sex is essentially an exercise in learning to read and care about another human's experience. This book encourages readers to consider the thoughts, feelings, and values of everybody involved in a sexual situation, and not to let their own thoughts, feelings, and values be compromised in order to fulfill someone else's expectations.

COURAGE. It's not always easy to speak openly about what you want and don't want when it comes to sex. Many of us have received societal messages that might be completely opposed to our inner truths. This book advocates honoring those truths, in yourself and in your partner, above all the other noise.

THIS BOOK IS NOT ABOUT:

ABSTINENCE ONLY. If you choose not to have sex, that is perfectly wonderful. This book is still a good resource for you; it can help you make that choice from an informed perspective, and it can help you be a good friend to those who choose otherwise.

ADVANCED ANATOMY. The human body is absolutely incredible, and there are many resources that can help you learn more about anatomy and the mechanics of sex. This book is more about building a healthy relationship to sex and sexuality.

MASTURBATION. Sex with yourself is often a great way to explore your sexuality at your own pace and learn about what you like and don't like, but partnered sex is the focus of this book.

LEGAL DETAILS. Laws about drinking age, what constitutes pornography, age of consent, and so on vary from state to state and country to country. This book won't go into detail about laws or legal definitions, focusing instead on the spirit and philosophy behind the concepts discussed. Realistically speaking, laws don't always control human behavior, and it's better to discuss sex out in the open than to obscure it and let people encounter it without education or knowledge of safe practices.

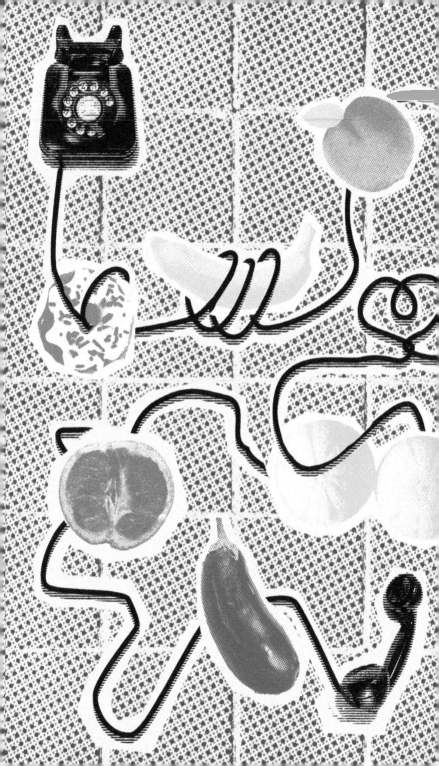

let's talk about sex

When people talk about sex, they're talking about a lot of different things: desire, intimacy, pleasure, and, of course, the physical act itself. But because sex is often such a taboo topic, there's a lot of misinformation about it out there. What you read on the internet or see in porn isn't always accurate. This chapter will cover the basics of sex: what it is, how it feels, and what all that means for you and your life. Let's start by separating sexual fact from sexual fiction.

FICTION VS. FACT: ALL ABOUT SEX

FICTION: *Everyone is doing it.*

FACT: The average American has sex for the first time around age 17, and about 62 percent of high school seniors report that they have had sex. That means that 38 percent—well over a third—of high school seniors have not had sex. So lots of teens are doing it, but certainly not everyone.

FICTION: *Kids are having more sex at younger ages these days.*

FACT: The number of teens who have sex before age 15 has actually declined in recent years. Their number of partners has remained about the same, though it is true that they're less likely than before to be in committed relationships with these partners.

FICTION: *Size matters.*

FACT: A lot of time and emotional distress is wasted by boys and men fretting about their penis size. Despite what you may see if you watch porn, the average erect penis is five to seven inches—but science shows us that for most people, the penis size of their partner has little to do with their sexual satisfaction. Much more important are things like length and quality of foreplay, and feelings of connection and acceptance.

FICTION: *Most women achieve orgasm from vaginal penetration.*

FACT: This is another thing porn portrays unrealistically. Very few women consistently achieve orgasm from vaginal penetration alone. Most women are their most orgasmic with stimulation of the vulva (the external part of female genitals), particularly the clitoris.

FICTION: *The word* virginity *has a generally accepted meaning.*

FACT: It is nearly impossible for people to agree on the meaning of the term *virginity*, because the concept is subjective. Many girls have broken their hymen by doing sports, masturbating, or using tampons, years before they have any kind of sex. Oral sex, anal sex, and vaginal penetration with a sex toy are all practices that might constitute "loss of virginity" to some folks but not to others. There really is no scientific definition of virginity. It's a cultural construct that has different meaning and value for different people.

FICTION: *If a man pulls out, a woman won't get pregnant, and an STI can't be transmitted.*

FACT: There are many infections that can be passed through skin-to-skin contact and have nothing to do with semen. Likewise, millions of sperm can be found in pre-ejaculate (the small amount of fluid emitted through the urethra of the penis before ejaculation), and it can be difficult to time pulling out correctly in the heat of the moment. The pull-out method has a much higher failure rate than any other form of contraception: about 22 percent of women using this method will get pregnant within a year.

FICTION: *Men can't be raped.*

FACT: Rape refers to nonconsensual sex, and has nothing to do with physiological markers of "arousal," such as the presence of an erection or vaginal lubrication. If he didn't want to do it and didn't give active, affirmative consent (or was underage, or too incapacitated by drugs or alcohol to give consent), it was rape. Approximately 12 to 15 percent of men report experiencing sexual assault in their lifetimes.

continued >

FICTION: *Women are more likely to be bisexual than men.*

FACT: Men are actually just as likely as women to be bisexual. Our culture, however, is much more accepting of women expressing bisexuality. Many surveys reflect this, with a slightly higher percentage of women than men identifying as bisexual (5 percent vs 2.5 percent). However, over 6 percent of men report that they have had oral or anal sex with another man.

FICTION: *Two condoms are better than one.*

FACT: Condoms are designed and engineered to be used one at a time. Putting one over another actually makes you less safe, because the condoms are more likely to rip. Check your condom for any evidence of damage, make sure the expiration date has not passed, and use it properly for the entire sexual encounter. If used this way, a single-layer condom is an excellent barrier method for preventing both pregnancy and most STIs.

FICTION: *Good sex should be like porn.*

FACT: Most pornography is fake: fake lighting, fake camera angles, fake editing. Remember, porn actors are just that: actors. Real sex often doesn't look or sound all that much like porn. Most importantly, good sex is equitable, respectful, consensual, and pleasurable for all involved, which unfortunately is not the case in a lot of porn.

What Is Sexuality?

What is this complex thing we call human sexuality? It's actually a combination of several elements that are blended and balanced in a way that is unique to every individual and varies over the course of one's lifetime.

SEX IS PHYSICAL. It involves the physical body, including but not limited to the genitals, the mouth, the breasts and nipples, and other "erogenous zones" (extra sensitive parts of the body). Expressing your sexuality with another person usually involves physical contact with each other's bodies in a way that feels pleasurable.

SEX IS CHEMICAL. Sure, sex hormones such as estrogen, progesterone, and testosterone are involved in sexuality. But so are hundreds of other chemical compounds that circulate in the brain and body, such as oxytocin, dopamine, and serotonin, to name just a few. Nitric oxide helps fill the erectile tissues in genitalia with blood, while pheromones transmitted through the air can attract a partner. Even the proteins and lipids excreted by bacteria on our skin—better known as "body odor"—can be a turn-on to the right nose.

SEX IS EMOTIONAL. Emotions related to sex, such as love, happiness, sadness, and jealousy (the list goes on), can all come into play to varying degrees and at varying times, even within a single relationship. All of these feelings can dramatically impact the expression of our sexuality, influencing key components such as sexual desire.

SEX IS SOCIAL. Humans have evolved to live and function in groups, and many of our behaviors are driven by a desire for acceptance, status, affection, or support. Sexuality is no different. It's one of many ways humans can engage with each other, and sexual relationships can be as significant as relationships with family and friends.

SEX IS CULTURAL. The culture you grow up in plays a key role in how you view sex and sexuality. Some cultures have strictly defined patterns of behavior regulating sexual expression, while others are freer and more accepting of individual differences and preferences. All of these approaches can incorporate healthy and positive sexuality, as long as individuals are not coerced or otherwise forced into sexual behaviors they don't want, or barred from consensual acts they do want.

SEXUALITY, AGENCY, AND POWER

We all have bodies. As we grow and develop from childhood through adolescence into adulthood, we have increasing amounts of agency to determine what we do with these bodies. Parents of a toddler might hold their child firmly so a doctor can administer a shot, for instance, but this same action would be nearly unthinkable for an adolescent of 15, and for a competent adult, it would be considered assault.

Expressing your sexuality is no different. As you become a young adult, you become responsible for your actions and choices. Some people choose to be sexual with another person only after marriage. Others choose to have multiple sexual partners over the course of a lifetime. Some may have long-standing intimate relationships, and some may have a lot of hookups or other sexual encounters with little to no emotional connection. Many go through combinations of all of the above.

You have the agency to make choices about your own body and self-expression. You have the power to say yes or no to sexual behaviors and encounters. No one else gets to decide those things for you, and you don't get to decide them for anyone else.

Making Sense of the Messages

We start picking up cultural messages about sex and gender roles when we are very young, and they have a huge impact as we get older and start to learn about and express our sexualities.

FAMILY. The first (and, some would argue, most potent) influence on our sexuality comes from the family unit. Do the parental figures in a family talk about sex as something potentially dangerous, potentially beautiful, or both? Or maybe they don't talk about sex at all. If a parent gives a child negative or positive messages about, say, being gay, that will have a profound impact on the child's views about their own orientation. Parents are the first educators on this subject, so if they can't discuss sexual issues openly in an age-appropriate way, children are likely to arrive at new experiences unprepared to make healthy, informed choices.

FRIENDS. As you move from childhood into adolescence, friends and peers start to have a greater impact on your thoughts and behavior. Many kids feel alienated or abandoned by their friends if their own sexuality doesn't align with what their peer group finds acceptable. But friends and peers are often supportive, too. Sharing your feelings and experiences with a friend who's your age and knows exactly what you're going through can be very comforting. Just remember, your friends don't get to decide if, when, or how you have sex—you do. Bullying does happen, especially toward LGBTQ youth, who are five times more likely to commit suicide than their straight classmates. If you feel there isn't a sympathetic friend or trusted adult around, please make use of one of the many free and anonymous call or text lines available in the Resources section of this book (page 103). You are not alone.

MEDIA. Sex is a weird subject in modern American culture. It is at once everywhere and nowhere. You can see blatantly sexualized images on billboards as you drive to a school that allows only abstinence-based sex education. Girls are valued for their sexual attractiveness but penalized for expressing their sexuality, while boys are pressured into the role of sexual aggressor but often receive no formal instruction on the importance of consent. It's not fair. And yet it's still our responsibility to sort through the mixed messages and express our sexuality in healthy and positive ways.

PORNOGRAPHY. In the vacuum of education on the subject, many people encounter their first images of sex through online pornography. It's available on any mobile device, it's free, and all it requires is the ability to type "sex" into a search bar. In fact, the average age when Americans are first exposed to pornography is between 13 and 14 years old. Natural curiosity leads kids down the online rabbit hole, and they're often left alone to make sense of what they find there. Unfortunately, what they find is usually unrealistic and often very unhealthy.

WHAT ARE SEXUAL PRESSURES?

Sexual pressures can be both internal and external.

Internal pressures come from our own internalized belief systems that tell us what is okay or appropriate to express with another person. A boy might think he *should* want sex or that he's not masculine enough if he doesn't have sex, even if no one has told him this directly. A girl might feel that it is somehow wrong or dirty of her to want sex, even if she watches movies and TV shows where women have plenty of sex. We absorb mixed messages from so many sources that it can be hard to sort out what our own beliefs and values are.

External pressures come from the outside, like when a group of friends exerts peer pressure to try to influence your behavior, or when a partner tries to get you to do something you're not comfortable with. Learning to dial into your own thoughts, feelings, and belief systems is essential to sorting out which pressures are coming from which places. Somewhere under there is your own unique, authentic truth. Acting in a way that aligns with that truth is what we call a healthy sexuality.

What Is Sex Like?

The way scientists describe what sex feels like has varied over the years. In their landmark book, *Human Sexual Response*, published in 1966, pioneering sex researchers William Masters and Virginia Johnson described a four-stage "sexual response cycle" consisting of *excitement, plateau, orgasm,* and *resolution.* Soon afterward, feeling it was essential to include the psychological, emotional, and cognitive contributions to the sexual response cycle, sex therapist Helen Singer Kaplan proposed a three-phase model: *sexual desire, excitement,* and *orgasm.* Other researchers object to using a linear model at all, and advocate for a circular model.

In plain terms, sex goes like this: When you're aroused, blood rushes into your genitals, leading to lubrication and/or increased sensitivity and pleasure in that area. As you have sex or are otherwise stimulated, these sensations build and build, until you experience the involuntary rhythmic contractions of pelvic muscles and pleasurable release of tension known as an *orgasm.* From there, you can either repeat the cycle with multiple orgasms (this tends to be easier for cisgender females than for cisgender males) or slowly return to a baseline non-aroused state, gradually becoming less sensitive and stimulated.

Everyone will have a slightly different experience of the sexual response cycle. It can change from partner to partner or even encounter to encounter with the same partner. There are no rights or wrongs, no normal or abnormal, so long as the experience is pleasurable and consensual.

Realistic Expectations about Sex

Most people have a learning curve when it comes to sex. The first several times you have sex are likely to be pretty awkward, and that's okay! Through trial and error, as you grow in maturity and self-confidence, you'll learn how best to give and receive pleasure. Hopefully, you'll move through this learning curve with positive and supportive partners who honor your comfort level at every step along the journey.

Real sex usually doesn't look anything like the sex you've seen in porn. That sex is a performance put together by actors, directors, and editors. Trying to learn about sex by watching porn is kind of like trying to learn how to perform heart surgery by watching *Grey's Anatomy*.

Real sex can look like a lot of different things, so it's best to let go of expectations and simply be present in the moment. Keep checking in with yourself and your partner about what you both want and what feels good, and chances are you'll figure it out in a way that is mutually enjoyable.

Most dates with guys typically end in sex, even though I'd prefer not to. Sometimes it just seems like that is all everyone looks for. —JEREMY, 23

Jeremy is expressing a common theme: having sex because he believes it's what his partners want or expect, not because it's what he truly desires. It may also be possible that his partners are doing exactly the same thing—acting in a way they believe they are expected to act. Take the time to check in with yourself and consider what it is that you truly want. If your partner's desires or priorities don't align with your own, then it's perfectly okay to walk away from that situation. As long as everyone is honest and respectful of each other, no one's bodies or feelings will get hurt, and we have space to find that partner with whom we do align.

WHAT IS SEXY?

So many people are caught up in insecurities, feeling ashamed or embarrassed that their body doesn't measure up to the "ideal." This is unfortunate, because, despite what you may see in the media and in porn, there is no such thing as a universally accepted ideal body type. Likes and dislikes, preferences and turn-ons are as broad and varied as snowflakes in a snowdrift.

In truth, the sexiest person is someone who's comfortable in their own skin, genuinely knows what they want, and is not afraid to ask for what feels good. The best way to relax and enjoy a sexual encounter is to own your unique beauty and trust that the right partner will appreciate and desire you for yourself.

Setting Limits and Boundaries

One of the most important things you need to learn as you start to become sexually active is how to set and respect boundaries regarding activity that you want and don't want. This is as important for boys as it is for girls, and both boys and girls can feel pressured into ignoring their own desires in order to fulfill social expectations. The best way to set these limits is for both partners to communicate clearly and freely in an ongoing way about what they want and don't want, what they're comfortable with, and what limits they want to set.

Regardless of your gender or your partner's gender, you always have the right to say, "Stop," "No," "I'm not comfortable with this," "I like this, but not that," or "I want to do that instead of this." Even if you've already started doing the thing you're uncomfortable with, or have done it before, you always have the right to stop at any time.

Likewise, regardless of your gender or your partner's gender, it is always your responsibility to listen for and respect your partner's limits, and not do anything they don't consent to. Sometimes people don't know how to clearly set boundaries and will communicate them indirectly with body language (stiffening up, looking away) or by talking about something else ("It's getting late"). If a boundary is not clearly articulated, that doesn't mean you have consent by default. It means you have to ask your partner what they want and don't want before moving forward.

I was hanging out with my friend who I knew liked me, and he kissed me but I didn't know how to stop him because I was worried about making him feel bad.

—CELIA, 14

There will be times in your life when you need to set boundaries or limits, and the result may be that your partner feels bad. This is just a part of life. Ultimately, you are doing your partner a huge favor by communicating honestly and with integrity about your true feelings. They need to learn that their desires may not always be mutually shared. You have to live with yourself, and compromising yourself to please another person is a self-sabotaging and unhealthy pattern to practice. It's better to practice self-love and self-compassion.

Choosing Not to Have Sex

Not having sex is a perfectly valid choice, and people make that choice for many different reasons. Some might have a moral or religious belief that sex should only happen in marriage or for the purpose of procreation, while others would like to have sex but haven't yet found the right person. For some people who have experienced sexual trauma, sexual activity triggers negative feelings (or even physical pain) that they would rather avoid. Some simply don't see sex as a priority and are focused on other goals like school or a career. Additionally, about 1 percent of the US population identifies as "asexual," meaning they don't feel sexually attracted to others, regardless of gender.

You can choose not to have sex at any time, even if you've had sex before. It's just as valid a choice as having sex, and it must be respected. If someone chooses not to have sex and someone else tries to manipulate or coerce them into it, gives them drugs or alcohol to incapacitate them, or forces sex on them, that is considered sexual assault or even rape.

CHAPTER 2

dating & relationships

Whether you call it "dating," "going out," "hanging out," or something else, getting together with another person in a romantic or sexual way is a normal part of adolescence and young adulthood for many people. This chapter will discuss relationships in their many forms and variations, breaking down some of the most common scenarios that can come up and healthy ways of handling them.

What's a Relationship?

Relationship is a term that describes the way two people are connected. There are many levels of emotional connection between people. At the lower levels, you'd find perfect strangers with zero emotional ties, acquaintances, or casual friends, while the higher levels would include close friends, family members, and love relationships. There are also many levels of physical connection. There are some people you'd feel comfortable shaking hands with or lightly hugging when saying hello or goodbye, some with whom you might want closer and prolonged physical contact, and some with whom you have very intimate contact, like kissing or sex. A relationship can be any combination of physical or emotional connection to another person.

HOW TO PROTECT YOURSELF WHILE ONLINE DATING

Online friendships and romantic connections can be just as intimate and real as offline ones, but sometimes people take advantage of the internet's anonymity to hurt others. Usually, meeting someone from the internet works out just fine. You don't need to be paranoid—just be smart. Until you get to know someone outside a dating app or social media site, it's wise to take these basic precautions:

- Don't send naked pictures of yourself to someone you don't fully trust. If you're under 18, it's best not to send them at all—depending on where you live, it may actually be a crime.

- Meet in a public space, and let people (like your parents or friends) know who you're meeting, where you're meeting, and what your plans are for the date.

- It's not wrong to snap a picture of your date when they show up and send it immediately to a parent or friend.

- If you're under 18, it's best not to meet someone who is more than a couple years older or younger than you are. If they lied about their age, it's a red flag that they may not have the best intentions.

- It's a good idea not to drink alcohol the first few times you're meeting someone new. It inhibits your ability to pick up on warning signs and exit the situation quickly and safely if you need to.

What Is Dating?

When you're interested in someone as a possible sexual or romantic partner, you might arrange to spend some time with them and see what happens.

You might go on a casual, cheap date where you grab coffee at a café, or on a more expensive and involved date, like going out to a fancy restaurant or spending a day at a music festival. You might know very little about the person you're meeting, beyond their online dating profile or a friend's description, or maybe you've exchanged some text messages and decided that you want to see what it feels like face-to-face. Sometimes your date might be a friend you know well, and you're just exploring a new energy that has entered the relationship. Some dating leads to a committed, long-term relationship, but plenty doesn't.

The most important constant in all these maybes and sometimeses is that you can never make any assumptions about what kind of sexual activity may or may not happen on a date. Just because someone you've been texting (or even "sexting") with agrees to meet, that doesn't mean sex is necessarily going to happen. Even if you spend a lot of money buying dinner for your date, you don't get to expect sex in return. Before anything sexual happens, everybody must be clear about what they want and what they feel comfortable with.

I sent a photo of me partially naked to a guy, and his friend took a picture and showed it to everyone. I felt exposed and shamed. No one wants to be the one whose nudes got leaked. —CAMILLE, 16

It's unfortunate, but sometimes the people we feel we should be able to trust most will abuse that trust. When you share a photo digitally, you have no control over what happens to it; it could be shared accidentally or maliciously. Nude photos, particularly if you are under the age of 18, should probably not be sent to anyone. As wrong as it may sound, all of the players in this scenario (even Camille herself) could potentially be charged with online distribution of child pornography. Obviously, not a great way to begin young adulthood.

Intimate Relationships

An intimate relationship is one in which you and another person share significant pieces of yourself. You know personal, important things about each other, and you genuinely care about each other's well-being.

An intimate relationship takes time to build. It's a gradual process of unveiling yourselves to each other, influencing each other, and growing together. In this process, it's essential to have a healthy foundation of trust. You're honest about your thoughts and feelings, and you listen to the other person's thoughts and feelings without rushing to anger or judgment.

Intimacy is also mutual. It's not like with a counselor or coach, where you talk about yourself and they listen and give feedback. In true intimacy, both partners become vulnerable, and trust, caring, and knowledge of intimate details run both ways.

Often, as two people in a relationship become more intimate, they'll agree on some kind of commitment to be romantically involved only with each other. (But it's also fine to be physically and emotionally intimate with more than one person, as long as everyone involved is open and honest about their feelings and actions.)

Intimacy doesn't have to involve sex, but when it does, people sometimes find that they have intimate knowledge of each other only physically, without other components like trust, mutuality, and commitment. That's not necessarily a bad thing, but it can be a pretty emotionally confusing situation. Only you know what feels right for you, but in those cases when you get the whole package—physical *and* emotional intimacy—it's pretty magical.

Open Relationships

An open relationship is one in which two partners agree that while they share physical and/or emotional intimacy with each other, they may also share it with others. It's *not* an open relationship if one partner is "allowed" to see other people and one is not. That's abuse and control.

The key to an open relationship is that everything is clearly out in the open, no one is hiding or obscuring behavior, and everyone involved has consented to this plan without threats, ultimatums, manipulation, or coercion of any type. It's a very mature and challenging type of relationship, even for experienced adults, as it requires rigorous honesty on a daily basis and immense courage to speak up about your thoughts and feelings as they arise.

Friends with Benefits

Friends with benefits are friends who have sex with each other but aren't interested in the full intimacy of a committed relationship with each other. In this kind of relationship, you might enjoy hanging out, share common interests, and care about each other as friends do, but you agree not to take on any emotional weight beyond a normal friendship.

As with open relationships, a friends-with-benefits situation can be challenging even for experienced adults. It's often difficult to separate physical intimacy from emotional intimacy. Just make sure everyone is on the same page. Both people should be open about their emotions and intentions and should consent to the relationship without any kind of coercion.

AM I READY TO HAVE SEX?

How do you know when you're ready to have sex? This is a really hard question. You might think you're ready, and yet your first sexual experience can teach you things about yourself you'd never have guessed beforehand. Answer the following questions to gauge whether you're ready to have sex.

1. Can you speak openly and without shame with your partner about your wants, needs, desires, and boundaries?

2. Do you feel comfortable walking into a drugstore and openly purchasing condoms and lubricant? Do you know the proper way to use a condom?

3. Do you feel comfortable talking to your doctor or health care provider about pregnancy prevention and STI testing?

4. Can you say no when you mean no, and yes when you mean yes? Can you say these things clearly out loud, and feel comfortable sticking to your decision even if your partner were to subtly (or not so subtly) pressure you?

5. Can you imagine being physically intimate with someone while having a clear and alert mind, without the need to be drunk or high in order to "get through it" and without feeling self-conscious or ashamed?

6. Do you understand that having sex with someone doesn't make them "yours" or prevent them from breaking up with you?

7. Do you really understand the mechanics of what sex is, including your own anatomy, your partner's anatomy, and how they interact?

8. Have you experimented with masturbation or self-touch? Do you know what you like and what feels good?

9. Are you prepared for the possibility that the experience might not go the way you imagine it will? Do you have a support system you can lean on to help you process your emotions as you go through this experience?

10. Can you trust your partner to respect your thoughts, feelings, and ownership over your own body, and to not abuse this incredible privilege? Can you trust yourself to do the same for them?

Did you answer yes to all? Even most sexually experienced adults can't answer yes to all 10. The truth is, you get as prepared as you can. If you examine your motivations, your physical readiness, your emotional stability, the quality of your relationship with a potential sexual partner—in short, if you approach the topic of sex from an educated and mindful place—you're off to a great start.

WHAT A HEALTHY RELATIONSHIP LOOKS LIKE

A romantic relationship can take many forms, from friends with benefits to decades of marriage. But whether your relationship is casual or committed, long-standing or brand-new, it should still be healthy.

Overall, a healthy relationship brings you joy, pleasure, excitement, new experiences, and personal growth. An unhealthy relationship resembles this, but overall it brings you more pain, anxiety, jealousy, fear, and personal stagnation. No relationship is perfect, and even the best ones involve some minor level of conflict or disagreement. But in a healthy relationship, conflicts give you the opportunity to practice good communication and conflict-resolution skills—they do not provide ammunition to hurt and manipulate each other.

Here are some hallmarks of a healthy relationship:

- **MUTUALITY.** Both people enjoy and want to be in the relationship. No one is in the relationship because of guilt or obligation.

- **HONESTY.** You can and do share your feelings with your partner without fear of judgment or reprisal.

- **SUPPORT.** Both people want good things to happen to each other and help each other make those good things happen.

- **RESPECT.** Partners see each other as equals and don't try to belittle each other, make each other feel bad, or control each other's actions.

- **COMPROMISE.** In a disagreement, you can meet your partner halfway, because you both trust each other to be honest and look out for each other. If one person usually has to be the one to compromise, or if one person wants the other to compromise on something critical to their sense of identity, that's not healthy.

- **NO ABUSE.** A healthy relationship never, ever involves verbal or emotional abuse, physical harm, or forcible or coercive sex.

Dealing with Rejection

Sooner or later, we all end up wanting someone who doesn't want us back. Whether someone turns you down when you ask them out or breaks up with you after several months or years of dating, it always hurts. It can be a massive blow to your self-esteem, and you may feel humiliated, unattractive, or unlovable.

However, those feelings aren't based in fact! Rejection is not a verdict on your worth as a person. It's a normal part of life that happens to everyone. You'll never meet an adult who hasn't had their heart broken (and if you did, that in itself would be sad, because it would probably mean they hadn't felt deep romantic love, either).

If a relationship isn't mutual, it's not a healthy relationship. You can and will find someone who's a better fit for you.

In the meantime, mourn the loss and allow yourself to feel all the feelings that come up. You have every right to feel sad and hurt! (But, you do *not* have the right to lash out at or try to punish the person who rejected you.) When the time is right, you'll find that your light shines even brighter than before, because you have learned and grown.

Breaking Up

So you've decided you want to break up with the person you're going out with. There are responsible and irresponsible ways of making this happen. A healthy relationship is based on trust, respect, and honesty. Maybe you want to end your relationship because you feel your partner didn't live up to these principles, but *you still can.* You can't control the emotions your partner will experience when you leave them, but you can control your own behavior. Your partner is almost certainly going to feel sad, hurt, and angry. But if you break up with them with integrity and compassion, you'll feel like you did the best you could, instead of feeling like a total jerk.

WHAT TO DO: Sit down with your partner face-to-face, and tell them that you no longer want to be together. Be clear and honest, but remember that you don't owe them an explanation. In fact, if you try to give them an explanation, they might try to argue with it, or they might feel you're attacking who they are as a person. Wanting to break up is the only reason you need to break up. It will probably be hurtful to them to hear this, but overall, it's the kindest way to go.

WHAT NOT TO DO: Assuming you've been going out with your partner for more than a few days, probably don't break up with them by text. Don't tell them a list of things they did wrong or things you don't like about them. Definitely don't keep your dissatisfaction to yourself and then cheat on them so that you have an excuse to break up—then they'll feel lied to and betrayed on top of everything else, and you'll feel guilty and mean. And, remember, don't let your partner's hurt feelings make you abandon your truth. If you've given it thought and concluded that the relationship should end, then you have the right to end it. Just try to do it clearly and definitively.

The first guy I dated cheated on me with some other guy he met online. We were about three months in when I found out. He asked me to stay, but I couldn't be around him anymore. For almost a year I wanted to talk to him again, but I told myself I'd never go back to someone who'd treat me like that. —JEREMY, 23

Being cheated on never feels good. Cheating can also lead to being exposed unwittingly to STIs, and with certain viruses, this could be extremely serious. Make sure you are in agreement with your partner about the exclusivity of your relationship, and don't make any assumptions. On top of that, discuss your expectations around honesty as well. Let them know that if something happens or changes for them in the relationship, you would rather talk about it than keep it secret. Once trust is violated, it can be difficult (though not impossible) to reconstruct. Know that you deserve to be treated well, with honesty and respect. The right partner will give you these things and more. Don't compromise yourself for someone who is operating out of pain and fear.

WHAT'S YOUR LOVE PERSONALITY?

What's your personal style when it comes to love? Take this quiz alone or with your partner to find out. Talking about your answers can lead to a deeper understanding of each other's needs and styles of expression and communication.

CATEGORY A:

1. I feel comfortable going directly for what I want and telling someone I like or love them. If they're not into it, that's fine. I'm not afraid to ask.

2. I check in with my own feelings and only do things sexually that I'm comfortable doing. No one's going to pressure me if I'm not ready.

3. I'm not overly concerned about what others think of me. I'll make my own choices and do what feels right, not what might make others like or approve of me.

4. I take the lead on planning fun things to do with my partner.

5. If we decide to have sex, I've done my homework. I know what I like and how to prevent unwanted pregnancy and STIs.

If you agree with more than three statements in this category, your love personality is Stable and Secure.

You're confident and grounded in yourself. You know that what others might gossip about has more to do with them than with you. You think about the well-being of yourself and others, and take an active role in any relationship. Just make sure you're leaving space for your partner's thoughts, feelings, and needs!

CATEGORY B:

1. I'm nervous to tell someone I like them because they might not like me back. I might pass a message through a friend because it feels less risky.

2. I can get carried away in a sexual situation and find myself doing things I don't really want to do. When someone is really into me, I don't want to hurt their feelings or disappoint them by saying no.

3. Being popular or getting praise from my family and friends is important to me. It would be devastating if I found out people were gossiping about me or saying mean things.

4. I'm pretty easygoing, and I want to make my sweetheart happy, so I leave planning dates and activities up to them. As long as they're having fun, I'm okay.

5. Sex feels like something that should just happen naturally. Planning too much will take the magic out of it. I trust my partner to tell me if they have an STI and to take precautions so we don't get pregnant.

If you agree with more than three statements in this category, your love personality is Shy and Sensitive.

You deeply care about others, sometimes to the detriment of yourself. At times you feel like other people's feelings are more important than your own. You are a giver and naturally trusting, so when someone doesn't act the way you expect them to, you might feel lost or betrayed. Remember that you are worthy of love and respect, and make sure that when being kind to others, you're not being unkind to yourself.

HOW TO GET OUT OF A BAD RELATIONSHIP

For the purposes of this section, "bad relationship" can mean anything from "not awesome" all the way to "outright abusive." People usually do the best they can with the emotional tool kit they have available to them at the time, but sometimes people can treat each other very badly. If you are being disrespected, lied to, controlled, or abused—physically, sexually, emotionally, or verbally—it's time to get out.

STEP 1: GET YOUR SUPPORT TEAM IN ORDER. Make sure you have a parent or trusted adult, as well as a good friend or two, who can be there to help you during this difficult time. They can listen to you nonjudgmentally, remind you you're loved, and help you stay true to yourself when things get murky.

STEP 2: TELL YOUR PARTNER YOU'RE BREAKING UP WITH THEM. If you feel physically unsafe, or if this partner has ever been violent to you (this includes sexual coercion or assault), you do not need to break up with them in person. Get yourself to a safe place, alert a responsible adult to the situation, and make sure you're never alone with the abusive person again.

STEP 3: TAKE CARE OF YOURSELF POST-BREAKUP. Try not to use other people, alcohol, or drugs as a way to distract yourself from unpleasant feelings. Eat well, exercise, and get good sleep. Use the time to reflect on what you've learned from this relationship. Identify things you'll look for in your next partner, and commit yourself to being an even better version of yourself next time around.

Your Relationship Doesn't Define You

We all have ways we tend to relate to other people, which psychologists call "attachment styles." These patterns are established in early childhood, influenced heavily by the kind of attachment an infant or young child has with a primary parent or caregiver. Below are the four major attachment styles, according to a study published in 1991 by researchers Kim Bartholomew and Leonard Horowitz in the *Journal of Personality and Social Psychology*. As you read about these styles, remember that humans have the remarkable ability to learn and grow through experience, self-reflection, therapy, and/or spiritual growth. Your current attachment style can and often does change.

ANXIOUS-PREOCCUPIED ATTACHMENT: You feel incomplete or empty without your partner. You need them to constantly validate you and your relationship, and any independence they show confirms your worst fears that they may leave you. Clingy and possessive behavior are hallmarks of this attachment style.

DISMISSIVE-AVOIDANT ATTACHMENT: You're emotionally distant and a bit shut down. You take care of yourself and your own needs, and pretend (or even truly believe) that you don't need anyone else. You walk away when things get too intimate or heated, and, on the surface, it may seem like it doesn't really bother you. This lets you temporarily avoid emotions about things like rejection and vulnerability, but you'll eventually have to reckon with them.

FEARFUL-AVOIDANT ATTACHMENT: The person you want to be consoled by is also the person you fear will hurt you the most. You can be moody, and you have emotional and unpredictable outbursts. You're afraid of being both too intimate with and too independent of your partner. Your relationships tend to have a lot of drama, as you erratically pull people in and then push them away.

SECURE ATTACHMENT: This is the one we're all aiming for. This style is equitable and honest, marked by the freedom to move independently in the world without fear of abandonment or loneliness. You trust your partner to be supportive and open, rather than cruel, manipulative, or thoughtless. You respect and admire your own and your partner's personal worth.

After a breakup, I went to a family friend who is a therapist and talked every week for two months. It helped. —ANDRE, 22

If we're open to receiving the messages, relationships usually teach us far more about ourselves than they do about the people we're with. We tend to find relationships that act out our thoughts and feelings about ourselves. If we believe we are unworthy of love, we tend to find people who prove that point. Processing a relationship post-breakup with a close friend, spiritual guide, or therapist can help us identify patterns of thinking and behavior and address them so that we aren't destined to repeat them next time around. It's normal to feel a range of emotions after a breakup. Practice good self-care, and know that the feelings won't last forever.

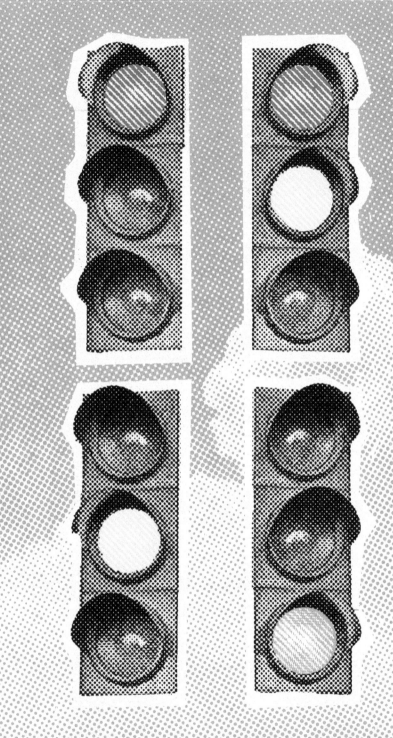

CHAPTER 3

consent, capacity, and communication

When it's good, sex can be wonderful and pleasurable, and it can increase your sense of joy and connection with others. When sex is bad, though, it can be really bad. Bad sexual experiences can have serious fallout, leading to trauma or even lifelong problems. This chapter will give you some essential tools so that, as you move into the world of sex, you increase the probability of joy and personal growth and decrease the chance of trauma and pain.

Consensual Sex

There's only one thing that's a must-have in every single sexual scenario, and that's consent. Consent is the shared responsibility of everyone who is engaging in (or wants to engage in) any kind of sexual interaction. Always make sure you have your partner's consent, and express to your partner that they have yours.

Consent begins with recognizing your own desires and then communicating them to your partner to see if they feel the same. It's not always easy. It might make you feel vulnerable. What if your partner isn't feeling it? What if you get rejected or your needs don't get met? Those can be scary possibilities—but not as scary as the possibility of sexual coercion or assault.

Consent has to be ongoing. Just because two people have sex once doesn't mean that either of them is obligated to have sex again, even if one of them wants to. In fact, if someone consents at the beginning of a sexual encounter, they can still withdraw consent later on in that same encounter. That's why it's important to keep checking in with each other to make sure everyone is still happy. This is part of the dance of sexuality. It is the constant tuning in to mutual wants and desires, so that everyone involved has the optimal experience.

Capacity

In order for someone to give consent, they have to have the *capacity* to do so. A yes isn't really a yes if a person isn't truly capable of giving it. Here are the factors that make it possible for someone to give real consent:

AGE

Are you and/or your potential partner under 18? If so, are you within two to four years of each other, age-wise? By law, children do not have the ability to give consent for sexual acts with adults, no matter how "mature" they may act or appear. Laws around age and consent differ according to what state (or country) you're in. To be safe, use common sense. If you're 17 years old with a driver's license, you're in a very different developmental place than a 13- or 14-year-old. It's best to choose partners who are on a level plane with you.

ABILITY

Are you and your partner of similar intellectual abilities? People with severe disabilities may not have the capacity to give sexual consent, like someone with a medical condition that impairs their ability to communicate their desires verbally or in writing, or someone with developmental disabilities whose intellectual age doesn't match their chronological age. It's always a good idea to check it out with a doctor or responsible adult before proceeding with any sexual interaction where there might be a mismatch of abilities.

POWER

In order for a yes to be meaningful, a no must be an equally acceptable option, with no negative consequences. Ask yourself: Is there a tilted power dynamic in the relationship? Does one of you have power or control over the other's physical or financial well-being? If your potential partner is your coach, teacher, boss, or anyone else in a position of authority, you may feel pressured to consent. You might worry that your boss will fire you if you don't consent, or hope your teacher will give you a better grade if you do. You might just do what they tell you to do because you trust them to have your best interests at heart or because you're used to a relationship in which they're the one giving you instructions. That's not true consent; it's coercion and abuse. It's always best to be on a level playing field with a sexual partner.

ALCOHOL/DRUGS

Are either of you using alcohol or recreational or prescription drugs that could affect your level of consciousness or memory? Alcohol is the most commonly abused substance when it comes to bad sex and lack of consent. If someone is in a significantly altered state of consciousness, is in a "blackout" state, or has passed out due to alcohol or drugs, *they cannot consent to any sex act*. This is true *even if they have previously given consent in the past*. Unfortunately, they may also be unaware that they are too intoxicated to consent, so it is everyone's responsibility to avoid any sexual contact with someone in this state. You may want to have sex, but you definitely don't want to commit sexual assault.

I started having sex fairly young. Most of those encounters were fueled by drugs and alcohol. There were times where I woke up and would not remember leaving the place with someone, how I got to where I was, and if we had sex or not.

Now, I do not drink as much as I used to, and the friends whose company I keep are responsible, respectable, and aware beings who do not take advantage of my body or mind. —MICHAELA, 20

Though she may not see it this way, Michaela is describing a history of multiple episodes of being victimized by "incapacitated rape," which is a sex crime. She describes something we call "voluntary incapacitation," a situation where she chose to drink alcohol or use drugs to the point of memory blackout, thereby losing the capacity to actually give consent to sex. The partners she was with may or may not have had any knowledge that they were committing a crime when they had sex with her, as she may have even given the impression that she was "consenting" to sex at this time.

The best way to handle this is to avoid sexual contact with anyone who appears overtly drunk or high. Likewise, take care of your friends if you see them getting to this point, and don't leave them alone. This may go against notions you've been told about partying, how to "score," or what kind of behavior you think you're supposed to participate in with your social group. As you can see from Michaela's story, she suffered from these early experiences and now sees how she was taken advantage of, harmed, and disrespected.

Words Matter

We may like to believe that we're masters at reading body language or facial expressions, but the truth is, lots of things can be misunderstood or misinterpreted, particularly if you don't know your partner very well. Adding alcohol or drugs to the mix only makes it that much harder to read and respond to each other's signals. The best way to keep things clear is by using words to both ask for and give consent.

Here are some things to keep in mind about verbal consent:

- IT APPLIES TO ALL GENDERS AND ALL ORIENTATIONS.

- IT'S AN ABSOLUTE MUST WITH FIRST-TIME PARTNERS AND IN NEW RELATIONSHIPS. You've never been here before with each other, so you can't assume anything and need to check everything out as you go. Even if you two have had sex a few times, you're still getting to know each other's likes and dislikes, erogenous zones and no-go zones. Until you have your sexual literacy with each other up to speed, it is always the right decision to explicitly ask. Even in established relationships, many couples use explicit verbal consent all or most of the time.

- **IT'S NECESSARY EVERY SINGLE TIME.** Don't assume that because it was a yes last weekend, it should be a yes again tonight. One of you might have been very enthusiastic the evening before but seriously not in the mood the morning after.

- **IT DOESN'T HAVE TO BE STILTED OR AWKWARD.** Checking in with your partner about what they like can be incredibly hot. It means you care about each other's pleasure, and what's hotter than that? If you don't feel comfortable speaking with someone about this, ask yourself if you should really be trusting them with intimate access to your body.

- **IT'S THE BEST AND EASIEST WAY TO CLARIFY NONVERBAL SIGNALS.** During a sexual encounter, you might notice your partner freezing or tensing up, going silent, turning their face away from you, or using their hand to guide you away from a certain area. When someone is using body language like that, just ask them about it! You can both use your words to get on the same page so that everyone is happy with what happens next.

CONSENT MAY SOUND LIKE . . .

Giving and receiving consent isn't a buzzkill or a formal contract that you have to sign. It's a two-way conversation—a call-and-response. You can talk about your own desire for a specific kind of touch as you ask your partner for their consent. A consent conversation can sound like a lot of different things. Here are some examples:

PERSON A: "You're so hot. I'd love to kiss you right now. Would you like that?"

PERSON B: "I think you're hot, too. I'd love to kiss you."

PERSON A: "I've been thinking about touching you all night. Do you want me to touch you? Take my hands and show me where you want to be touched."

PERSON B: "Mmm, yes, please. Touch me here . . . and here . . ."

PERSON A: "I want you so much. Do you want to have sex? Let's go however far you're comfortable with. You lead the way and show me what you want."

PERSON B: "I'm ready. I want to have sex with you, too. Let's not rush. I'll tell you what I like or if I want to do something different as we go."

NON-CONSENT MAY SOUND LIKE...

Because consent is a conversation between two people and not a formal contract, someone *not* giving consent doesn't always sound like, "No, I do not want to have sex with you." If a person doesn't say no, that doesn't mean they've consented by default. There are many ways not to give consent. Here's what some of those conversations can sound like:

PERSON A: "You're so hot. I'd love to kiss you right now. Would you like that?"

PERSON B: "I think it's better if we hang out sometime when you're not drinking and see how we feel then."

PERSON A: "I've been thinking about touching you all night. Do you want me to touch you? Take my hands and show me where you want to be touched."

PERSON B: "I think you're really hot, too. Let's just kiss for now. I'll let you know if I want your hands to go anywhere else."

PERSON A: "I want you so much. Do you want to have sex? Let's go however far you're comfortable with. You lead the way and show me what you want."

PERSON B: "I'm just not into it tonight. This doesn't feel right. Let's cuddle and watch the movie."

If someone doesn't consent to a sexual activity, they do not owe their partner apologies, explanations, or excuses. If you want something, say so. If you don't want something, say so. Sexually speaking, we don't owe each other anything other than mutual respect for each other's boundaries.

What Consent Is and Is Not

Exactly like a conversation, consent is ongoing and fluid. It requires speaking and listening, asking and responding. It can change direction at any moment. It can pause, become circular or redundant for a period of time, and then proceed. (And, like in a conversation, if you're drunk to the point of slurring your words or stumbling around, it's time to stop.) The most common phrase you hear about consent is "no means no," and that's very true. But there's so much more to it than that. For sex to be truly equitable, safe, and pleasurable for everyone, both partners need to give ongoing, clear, enthusiastic consent throughout the entire interaction.

Now that we know what consent is, here are a few things consent is not:

CONSENT IS NOT A BINDING CONTRACT. You can back out of it anytime you want to. Just because you said yes at one moment, that doesn't mean you're obliged to keep going if something doesn't feel right.

CONSENT IS NOT A "FREE PASS." If you have consented to oral sex, that doesn't mean you've automatically consented to vaginal sex. If you've consented to anal sex once, that doesn't mean you've automatically consented to do it again in the future. Consent is specific to the activity in the moment it is requested—only that activity and only in that moment.

CONSENT IS NOT EXCLUSIVELY ONE PARTNER'S RESPONSIBILITY.
Traditionally, sex between a guy and a girl has been framed as: he sees how far he can get, and it's up to her to set the limits. Not only is this outdated gender stereotyping, it also puts too much pressure on the guy to be the only one asking for consent, and too much pressure on the girl to be the only one setting boundaries. Both partners should share in making their own desires clear and listening to their partner's desires.

Giving Consent

When you give consent, you should be giving it freely and truly. If someone is asking for your consent for a specific sexual interaction, ask yourself these questions before you respond:

1. If this person is an adult, am I at least 18 years old? If we're both under 18, is there a big age gap between us?
2. Am I quite drunk or high? Is the world spinning? Do I feel sick?
3. Is my potential partner obviously drunk or high, and therefore more likely to ignore my desires and boundaries?
4. Do I really want to do this thing they're asking me to do? Would it be enjoyable for both of us, or just for them?
5. If I say yes, is it because I want to say yes or because I'm afraid to say no to this person?
6. What am I hoping or expecting will happen after I do this sexual thing they're asking for? Do I believe it will make the person "mine" or "bind them to me"? Will I be devastated if that doesn't come true?

The guy was someone I did not want to have sex with but did anyway. It wasn't good sex, and I felt gross/mad at myself afterwards. This happened years ago, but I still have to see him sometimes because his father is the owner of a restaurant I work at. I've only recently spoken about this situation to a friend/coworker when he was present at the restaurant and I had to serve him. —DARA, 20

It's unclear, but it's possible that Dara was working at the restaurant when her boss's son pursued her for sex. She may have felt that saying no would have endangered her job. Maybe she thought that saying no would be too complicated or make the guy angry. Maybe she believed it was expected of her. It's possible the guy Dara is describing had a pattern or history of preying on his father's employees, abusing this power for his own sexual agenda. Sexual coercion is on the spectrum of sexual assault, as by definition there is an absence of a clear, enthusiastic, affirmative consent.

Sex that comes after any kind of coercion usually isn't "good sex," and self-blame and feelings of self-disgust are normal responses. It's a type of trauma, and I hope very much that Dara finds the support she needs to begin the healing process. Sharing her experience with a trusted friend/coworker might be an important first step. The #MeToo movement moved like a tidal wave because survivors started talking to each other and let go of the guilt and shame they had held on to for so long.

Asking for Consent

When someone gives consent, they need to really mean it, not just give in because they've been pressured or misled. If you're interested in sexual activity with someone, ask yourself these questions before you ask for their consent:

1. Does my potential partner have the capacity to consent to sex?
   - Are they of legal age?
   - Are they obviously drunk or high?
   - Are they awake and alert?
   - Do they have a disability that could affect their capacity to consent?
   - Is there a power imbalance making them fear physical, social, or financial retribution if they say no?

2. Am I quite drunk or high? Is the world spinning? Do I feel sick?

3. Have I clearly stated my desires and asked my partner to tell me theirs? Are we on the same page about what we want to happen?

4. Have I been clear about what the proposed sexual activity would mean for our relationship, so that there are no misunderstandings about how casual or serious my partner and I feel this activity is?

5. What am I hoping or expecting will happen if we do this sexual thing? Do I believe that it will make the person "mine" or "bind them to me"? Will I be devastated if that doesn't come true?

Accepting and Respecting Non-Consent

When you ask for consent, you need to listen to and respect the other person's response. In healthy, consensual sex, you don't get to "make someone an offer they can't refuse."

Accepting and respecting non-consent without anger, resentment, or bitterness can be a really hard thing to do sometimes. When you reveal to someone that you want something that makes you vulnerable, and they tell you that they aren't willing to give it to you, it can bring up many difficult feelings. You may feel rejected, unworthy, unappreciated, unseen. You may feel embarrassed, humiliated, disappointed, frustrated, or even angry. You may feel the urge to retaliate or say something mean to the person to try to make them feel some of the same unpleasant emotions you're feeling.

Don't. Instead, acknowledge your own feelings and take care of yourself. It is not the job of the person who has not consented to take care of your feelings. They have their own feelings to take care of. Recognize that if consent is not given freely and enthusiastically, it is not actual consent. Do not try to pressure or manipulate them into giving you what you want when they've already said no. That's called sexual coercion, or even sexual assault. You really don't want to be that person.

STOP SIGNS

Sometimes you can be in the heat of the moment during sex and suddenly realize that something is very wrong with your partner. Sometimes you can be actively having sex and then start to feel less and less comfortable with what you're doing. Both of these scenarios are signs that you should immediately STOP and talk with your partner about how you're both feeling. If it turns out everything's cool, you can always pick up where you left off. What you can't do is take back selfish or uncaring behavior toward yourself or your partner.

Here are some signs you should stop having sex and ask for more information:

- One of you freezes up, stiffens, goes entirely limp, or becomes unresponsive

- Either one of you says any variation of "Wait," "Stop," "Don't," or "Hold up"

- You're in physical pain or your partner seems to be in physical pain

- The condom is no longer there. (If you consented to sex with a condom, and suddenly you realize the condom has been deliberately removed, that's not what you consented to, and it's not okay. It's sexual assault.)

- Your partner is saying things or doing things that make you feel disrespected or devalued, and you don't like it

- Someone starts crying

- Your partner has been vocal and encouraging up to a point, but then goes silent

BODY LANGUAGE AND CONSENT

Is body language a real language? Yes, actually. According to scientists, we do much of our communication nonverbally using body movements, facial expressions, and vocal tone. The problem is that body language is more open to misinterpretation than spoken language, and when it comes to sex, that can lead to a pretty bad situation. Alcohol and drugs make that situation even worse by impairing the parts of the brain that let us read other people's nonverbal cues. So when you're in a sexual situation, it's always wise to use your words to make sure everyone involved is happy with what's going on.

That being said, we do get to know each other during the course of intimate relationships. Longtime partners often get really good at reading each other's signals. If you've been in a sexual or romantic relationship with someone for a while, have an excellent system of verbal communication, and want to start relying more on nonverbal signs and body language during sex, that's totally fine. Pleasurable sounds, body movements that draw the other person closer, and deliberate guiding of your partner's mouth, hands, or genitals are great ways to communicate what you want and what feels good. Just be aware that if you notice something different or unexpected, you can never go wrong by using words to check it out— but you can go very, very wrong by choosing to ignore it.

Sex and Obligation

Sex can be kind of like a gift exchange: I do this for you, then you do this for me. That sounds fair and equitable, right? It can be, but it should also be completely and entirely voluntary and nonobligatory.

If we give, we must do so for the pleasure of the giving, without necessarily expecting reciprocity. If he wants to perform oral sex on you until you have a mind-blowing orgasm, that's fantastic. You do not owe him oral sex in return. She can treat you to a lovely and expensive romantic dinner at your favorite Italian restaurant, and you do not owe her sex in return. The only thing we ever owe a partner is respect for their boundaries.

Of course, if you're in an uneven relationship where one person does the majority of the giving, you may want to reevaluate whether you want to continue that relationship. But that does not mean you owe anyone any kind of sex, ever.

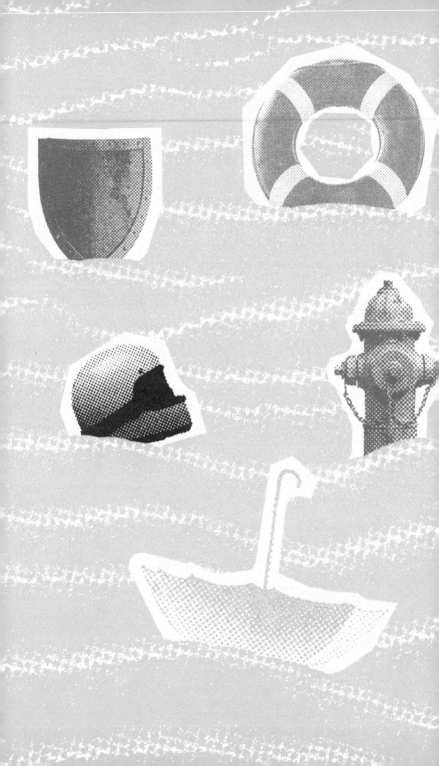

CHAPTER 4

practicing safer sex

As with many things in life, there's no such thing as completely and totally safe sex. All sex holds some inherent risks, be they emotional or physical. Talking about "safe sex" is kind of like talking about "safe skydiving." Yes, it can be thrilling and pleasurable, it can even be a celebration of life and humanity, but there are still certain risks. And just as you'd take precautions like wearing a parachute when skydiving, you can also take precautions to make sex less risky. This chapter is about "*safer* sex"—how to minimize as many of the risks as possible and have the best possible sexual experiences throughout your lifetime.

SAFER SEX: HOW MUCH DO YOU KNOW?

Take this quiz to see how much you know about safer sex.

TRUE OR FALSE? *You can't get a sexually transmitted infection (STI) unless you have sex with a lot of people.*

FALSE. Some people who have a lot of sex never get an STI, while some people who have only one partner in their entire life get an STI because that partner has been previously exposed. In fact, it's technically possible to get an STI even if both partners are "virgins," because more than half the adults in the United States have oral herpes (the cold sores that people get on their mouths that have nothing to do with sex), which can be transferred to a partner as genital herpes during oral sex. Condoms greatly reduce but don't fully eliminate the risk of exposure to STIs. The point is: STIs are incredibly common, they can happen to anyone, most are treatable, and getting one doesn't mean you're promiscuous or a bad person.

TRUE OR FALSE? *Condoms are an excellent birth control method when used properly.*

TRUE. With perfect use, condoms are 98 percent effective at preventing pregnancy. What is perfect use? That means you use a condom that is not past its expiration date, remove it from its package without using teeth or a sharp object, check it for damage, put it on before any genital contact occurs, use it for the entire duration of intercourse, use water-based (not oil-based) lubricant to prevent tearing, and discard it after one use. Unfortunately, most people don't use condoms perfectly. In typical use scenarios, condoms are only 75 to 80 percent effective. This is why it's a good idea to use a backup contraception method such as a birth control pill or an IUD in addition to a condom. Note that even with perfect use, there is still a 2 percent risk of pregnancy. Unintended pregnancy is a possible outcome of most heterosexual intercourse.

TRUE OR FALSE? *If you save your virginity for the person you truly love and who truly loves you, your heart won't be broken and you'll have no regrets about sex.*

FALSE. There are absolutely no guarantees in life or in sex. People grow, change, believe they want one thing and then come to discover that they want something else. It is possible to love someone very deeply and still end up breaking up with them. If your heart has the capacity to feel love, then it has the potential to feel pain. Of course, knowing and caring deeply for the person you choose to experience sex with for the first time can help avoid some communication hurdles, but it cannot protect you from heartbreak.

Sexual Health Care

When you begin to experiment with sexual activity, it's important to have a health care provider you can trust.

For girls in their early teen years, it's a good idea to make at least an introductory visit to a gynecologist or nurse practitioner who is comfortable working with adolescents. This establishes a relationship, making it easier for girls to reach out with questions about birth control methods and STI prevention early on, so they're prepared when they do start having sex later. Boys don't really have the same kind of long-term relationship with urologists (though perhaps they should), but they should still be able to talk to their doctor about the same issues. If you identify as transsexual or transgender, it is probably a good idea to find a health care provider who is familiar with caring for transsexual and transgender patients and will use sensitive and respectful language at every visit. I'm sorry if you've already had a bad experience. Please don't give up on finding the right provider and taking care of your health needs.

Parents should always give adolescents and their doctors a few minutes of time alone for sensitive questions to be asked, and should not insist that their kids report to them exactly what was discussed. This makes the relationship between a health care provider and an adolescent or young adult a safe place, and increases the likelihood that the patient will get scientifically accurate, unbiased information and effective risk-reducing tools.

STIs like chlamydia and gonorrhea are common enough that all sexually active people, regardless of gender, should get a routine testing once per year. It is also important to get tested for STIs any time you have a potential risk for exposure, like if a former partner lets you know they were just diagnosed with one.

Taking responsibility for your own sexual health is an important sign that you're ready for some of the complexities of being sexually active. If having an open conversation about sexual health with a doctor makes you feel uncomfortable, you probably shouldn't be engaging in sexual activities.

Preventive Measures

There are two main things you want to prevent during (consensual) sex: unintended pregnancy and STIs. Some safer-sex precautions protect you from one but not the other. Barrier methods are the only ones that prevent both. There are pros and cons to each method, and it's important to talk to a health care provider about which ones are right for you.

Note: When discussing birth control methods, people talk about *perfect use* versus *typical use*. Perfect use describes how effective a method would be if it were used perfectly every time, while typical use describes how effective it tends to be in real-world situations where people might make mistakes like using a condom past its expiration date or forgetting to take birth control pills. The effectiveness rates listed on pages 63 to 66 reflect typical use, not perfect use.

Before I have sex with anyone, I make sure to discuss STIs and try to make clear what I want out of the relationship or sex before it happens (without killing any sexual energy). I just like to be safe. Usually, if the person has had tests done and is negative for STIs, I'll say forget the condom, because of the birth control I use. There is usually never a big disagreement or issue with this topic for me. —MAYA, 20

Maya is a sexual rock star. She is thinking ahead, comfortable with speaking openly and clearly about her wants and desires, and even feels confident that she can do this without compromising any of the sexual energy in the relationship. She values herself and her own physical and emotional well-being, and she knows that she deserves to be with a partner who will do the same. She is doing the best she can to make smart choices. There are no guarantees that she will never encounter an STI or an unintended pregnancy, but her risks of doing so are significantly reduced.

BARRIER METHODS

Barrier methods provide a literal barrier between your skin and your partner's. This barrier protects against both STIs and pregnancy by preventing you from coming in direct contact with each other's bodily fluids and by keeping sperm away from eggs.

MALE CONDOM: A sheath made of latex or a similar material that goes over the penis during sex.

- 82 percent effective against pregnancy (with typical use)
- Very effective against STIs

FEMALE CONDOM: A sheath made of latex or a similar material that goes inside the vagina during sex.

- 79 percent effective against pregnancy (with typical use)
- Very effective against STIs

DENTAL DAM: A small sheet made of latex or a similar material that goes over the vulva during oral sex.

- Pregnancy prevention doesn't apply to oral sex
- Very effective against STIs

HORMONAL METHODS

These birth control methods use hormones like estrogen and progestin to keep a woman's body from ovulating, to thicken the cervical mucus to inhibit sperm from entering, or to create an inhospitable environment in the uterus for an embryo to implant (some have multiple or all of these effects). If ovulation doesn't occur, there is no egg for the sperm to fertilize, so pregnancy doesn't occur. It's important to consult with a doctor before using hormonal birth control methods, as they can cause side effects. Hormonal birth control only protects against pregnancy, not STIs.

THE PILL: A hormone pill taken around the same time every day.

- 91 percent effective (with typical use)
- Does not prevent STIs

THE MORNING-AFTER PILL: A hormone pill taken within a few days after having unprotected sex.

- 75 to 89 percent effective (with typical use)
- Does not prevent STIs

THE PATCH: An adhesive patch (kind of like a Band-Aid) that's applied to the skin. It secretes hormones, and is replaced once a week.

- 91 percent effective (with typical use)
- Does not prevent STIs

CONTRACEPTIVE RING: A flexible, hormone-secreting ring that's placed inside the vagina and replaced once a month.

- 91 percent effective (with typical use)
- Does not prevent STIs

SHOT/INJECTION: A hormone shot given by a doctor every three months.

- 94 percent effective (with typical use)
- Does not prevent STIs

ROD IMPLANT: A small, hormone-secreting rod that a doctor inserts into the skin, where it stays for up to four years.

- Over 99 percent effective
- Does not prevent STIs

IUDS: Short for intrauterine device, the IUD is a small T-shaped device that a doctor puts inside the uterus. Hormonal IUDs secrete hormones, but there are nonhormonal ones, too. They last 3 to 10 years, depending on the type and brand.

- Over 99 percent effective
- Does not prevent STIs

PERMANENT SURGICAL METHODS

These surgical pregnancy-prevention methods are for people who are very sure they don't want children, who already have children and don't want more, or who could have serious health risks if they got pregnant. These methods do not protect against STIs.

TUBAL LIGATION: A surgery that blocks the fallopian tubes so eggs can't travel into the uterus, where they can be fertilized. Colloquially known as "having your tubes tied."

- Permanent
- Over 99 percent effective
- Does not prevent STIs

VASECTOMY: A surgery that blocks the vas deferens in the scrotum so that sperm can't travel out of it. Sometimes it can be reversed, but it's considered more or less permanent.

- Permanent
- Over 99 percent effective
- Does not protect against STIs

OTHER METHODS

The following methods used to be more popular, but have become less so as contraceptive technology has advanced. They're a little harder to use and a little less effective than the methods previously discussed. Because they're less effective, they should always be used with a spermicidal (sperm-killing) lube or gel.

DIAPHRAGM (PLUS SPERMICIDE): A soft, flexible cup put inside the vagina to cover the cervix during sex.

- 88 percent effective (with typical use)
- Does not prevent STIs

CERVICAL CAP (PLUS SPERMICIDE): A soft, flexible cup put inside the vagina to cover the cervix during sex (similar to a diaphragm but with a slightly different shape).

- 71 to 86 percent effective (with typical use)
- Does not prevent STIs

CERVICAL SPONGE (PLUS SPERMICIDE): A small sponge put inside the vagina to cover the cervix during sex.

- 76 to 88 percent effective (with typical use)
- Does not prevent STIs

WHAT TO DO IF YOUR PARTNER REFUSES OR DISAGREES

Sometimes you might decide on a birth control or STI prevention method that feels right for you, only to find that your potential partner disagrees. They're allowed to have their own opinion. We can only make decisions for ourselves, and can never force those decisions on our partners. The good news is you get to have a conversation about it. Try to find out where your partner is coming from, what fears they have, and if they've been exposed to any inaccurate information or misconceptions.

Be gentle, be patient, but be clear. Above all, *never* compromise your safety, integrity, health, or well-being. If, after a conversation, you two still disagree on what kind of birth control or STI prevention method you want to use, then this is simply not a good partner for you right now. That's fine! Two people don't have to agree on everything—it's just that one can't pressure the other to have sex in a way they don't want to.

FACT OR FICTION: BEHAVIORS THAT CAN LEAD TO PREGNANCY

There's a lot of information floating around about what can and can't lead to pregnancy, and a lot of it is completely false. Here are some of those myths, debunked.

FICTION: *A woman can get pregnant from a toilet seat.*

FACT: A woman can only get pregnant when a sperm travels up the vagina, through the cervix, and into the uterus, where it meets an egg that has traveled down the fallopian tube. Even if there were sperm on a toilet seat, it would quickly die and would not be able to make the journey.

FICTION: *Pregnancy can be avoided by jumping up and down immediately after sex, douching after sex, or having sex with the woman on top.*

FACT: These are completely ineffective birth control methods. Sperm have little tails that let them swim upward, despite anyone's best attempts to jump, flush out, or otherwise discourage them from doing so.

FICTION: *If a guy smokes marijuana, he's less likely to get a girl pregnant.*

FACT: Weed is not a reliable form of birth control. It's true that marijuana might lower sperm count, but not so much that it can be relied upon to prevent pregnancy.

FICTION: *Pregnancy can't occur from anal sex.*

FACT: It's difficult to get pregnant from anal sex, because sperm can only reach the uterus from the vagina, not from the anus. But if any semen does accidentally get into the vagina during anal sex, it can result in pregnancy.

FICTION: *Pregnancy can occur from swallowing semen during oral sex.*

FACT: The mouth is not connected to the uterus, which is where the sperm fertilizes the egg, so there is no way of getting pregnant from swallowing sperm.

FICTION: *Peeing after sex prevents pregnancy.*

FACT: Urine comes out of the urethra, which is a completely separate tube from the vagina, so it has no effect whatsoever on whether sperm travel through the vagina to the uterus where they can fertilize an egg. Peeing *does*, however, flush bacteria out of the urethra, so peeing after sex is a good way to prevent a urinary tract infection (UTI).

FICTION: *The birth control pill is a foolproof method for preventing pregnancy.*

FACT: Unfortunately, there's no such thing as 100 percent foolproof birth control (except abstinence). If birth control pills are taken exactly as directed, at the same time every day, there's only a tiny chance (0.1 percent) that pregnancy will occur. But, in real life, pills can be accidentally left at home or people can forget to take them. With typical use, about 9 percent of women using the pill as their only birth control method will become pregnant within one year. Additionally, the pill and other hormonal contraceptives can be less effective for women classified as obese.

FICTION: *Pregnancy can't occur if a woman is on her period.*

FACT: False. Sperm can live for five days inside a woman's body before fertilizing an egg. So if a woman has sex near the end of her period and ovulates soon after that, the sperm could still be present to fertilize the ovulated egg and get her pregnant. It's safest to use a preferred form of contraception when having sex, regardless of where a woman is in her menstrual cycle.

Sexual Behaviors and Sexually Transmitted Infections

If you're sexually active, chances are that at some point in your life, you'll get an STI. It's like the common cold. If you're moving around on this planet, you're at risk for picking up viral and bacterial infections. Here's what you can do to deal with that:

BE PROACTIVE. Using condoms and other barrier methods during sexual activity is the safest and most effective way to keep from contracting an STI. If you're sexually active, get tested for common STIs once a year. Get vaccinated for STIs that have vaccines available, like human papillomavirus (HPV) and hepatitis B.

GET TREATMENT. If you do contract an STI, it's important to see your doctor as quickly as possible. This can dramatically reduce the risk of long-term consequences. Some STIs, like chlamydia, gonorrhea, and syphilis, are simple to treat if recognized early but can lead to much more complex problems if left untreated. Similarly, if you start post-exposure prophylaxis (PEP) within 72 hours of exposure to HIV, you might avoid permanently contracting the HIV virus. The earlier you start treatment, the better.

NOTIFY RECENT PARTNERS. Let your recent partners know that they may have been exposed to an STI and should receive testing and/or treatment. It's an awkward conversation, but plenty of us have had it. If you feel too uncomfortable, there are services that will send your partner an anonymous text or email.

DISCLOSE TO NEW PARTNERS. You owe it to yourself and to your sexual partners to disclose any STI you carry that they could potentially contract. This is basic good citizenship in the sexual world. If someone discloses an STI to you, please reward this gesture of courage and compassion by thanking them for their honesty and integrity. Don't leap to any negative judgments. People's assumptions about STIs are often much worse than the reality. Get all the information from them that you can, then have a discussion with a health care provider about how you and your partner can reduce the risk of transmission if you become sexually active with this person.

PREVENT TRANSMISSION. If you have an STI that is currently incurable, that doesn't mean you'll never have sex again. It just means you'll have to be honest with your partner and take steps to decrease the risk of passing it along. There are medications that dramatically reduce or even eliminate the chances of passing herpes or HIV to a partner.

STI RISKS

Nothing in this life is without risks, but when it comes to STIs, some activities are riskier than others.

LOW RISK

- Kissing.

- Grinding or fondling with clothes on.

- Digital stimulation of a partner's genitals (using your hands to touch their genitals).

- Masturbating or touching yourself with unwashed hands or sex toys can result in a UTI. The risk of STIs becomes greater if you're using a shared sex toy that hasn't been properly cleaned.

MODERATE RISK

- Oral sex *without* a barrier method such as a condom or dental dam can put you at risk for all of the same STIs as intercourse.

- Oral sex *with* a barrier method such as a condom or dental dam is much less risky, though viruses such as herpes and HPV can sometimes be transmitted through contact with parts of the genital region that aren't covered by a condom.

HIGHER RISK

- Penis-in-vagina sex can expose both partners to STIs. Using a barrier method like a condom makes it less risky. More lubrication also makes it less risky because it means the inside of the vagina is less likely to get tiny, microscopic cuts that make it easier to transmit blood-borne infections.

- Anal sex can expose the person in the "penetrating" or "top" position to blood and body fluids, particularly because of the thin, easily torn skin in the anus and rectum. Unlike the vagina, the anus doesn't naturally produce its own lubrication, which makes the pulling and tearing of skin (even microscopically) more likely to occur. Lubricant and condoms make anal sex much less risky.

VERY HIGH RISK

- The highest-risk sexual activity for STI transmission is anal sex in the "receiving" or "bottom" position. The delicate and easily torn skin in the anus and rectum can be a convenient entry point for an STI, whether it's a viral or bacterial infection. Because the anus doesn't naturally produce lubrication like the vagina does, it's even easier for that skin to get tiny, microscopic tears. Lubricant and condoms make anal sex much less risky.

How to Incorporate Safer Sex into Your Sex Life

The most important thing you can do to incorporate safer sex practices into your life is to have open and honest conversations with your partner about risk. To do this, take a curious and nonjudgmental approach to the conversation. Tell your partner that you're more interested in honesty and clarity than jealousy or judgment, and make it clear that you don't consider a history of an STI to mean your partner is somehow dirty or bad. (Would you judge them for telling you they once caught the common cold?) Ask about the last time they were tested for STIs, and tell them about the last time you were tested. Come up with a shared agreement about what kind of tools you want to use to make sex safer.

One of the most common roadblocks here is that one partner might not want to use a condom. Many people have misconceptions about condoms, thinking that sex won't feel as good or that you're not as intimate with your partner if you use them. In fact, sex can feel fantastic with a condom. The peace of mind you get knowing you're more protected from pregnancy and STIs goes a long way toward making both partners enjoy the experience and each other more. If you're serious and clear about wanting to have safer sex, chances are your partner will choose sex with a condom over no sex. And if they choose no sex, congratulations: you avoided having sex with someone displaying serious red flags about not respecting your safety or treating you well.

I've been in a situation where someone wanted to have sex without a condom, but I told him, "No glove, no love." He listened. —WHITNEY, 15

Most of the time you will find that being clear about your desires and boundaries is rewarded with your partner respecting those limits. Most people are honorable and want to be good to each other. Sometimes you will encounter someone who isn't and doesn't. Once you've cleared up any misconceptions or misunderstandings, if they maintain on this course of disrespect, I urge you to RUN, NOT WALK away from the interaction. Everyone you choose to gift with access to your sexuality should treasure that gift and take every precaution to honor and respect your wishes at all times. Whitney shows remarkable strength and poise in being able to communicate this clearly at age 15.

CHAPTER 5

abuse and assault

Abuse and assault can happen to anyone—of any class, race, gender, or sexual orientation. The same is true of those who commit abuse—they can be anyone. It is true that 90 percent of survivors of sexual assault are female, but that means there are plenty of males who also experience sexual violence. Sexual abuse and assault can be a vicious cycle in which those who abuse have also been abused. The good news is that, although our society's rates of sexual violence are unacceptably high, we are making progress, with overall rates of reported sexual violence declining over the past 20 years. The solution to this epidemic will have to be comprehensive and compassionate in order to make the world a safer and healthier place for all of us.

When I was 17, I was at a party where two guys made a bet with one of their friends. The details of the bet included touching and undressing me, even if I didn't agree. Luckily, I knew the boys well enough and noticed what type of situation I was in before it became severe, but I ended up having a panic attack. The way my mind received being treated like that was terrifying to me. —LAYLA, 18

Layla recognized that she was in a bad situation that had the potential to become even worse. She was targeted as a sexual object—her basic humanity and right to bodily autonomy was being compromised, and she felt threatened because she was being threatened. These boys made a terrible mistake believing that this was an acceptable course of behavior. If you happen to witness behavior like this or hear about it, be the stand-up person and intervene. We're all responsible for taking care of each other and setting the tone for what is okay and what is definitely #NotOK.

Legal Issues and Your Sex Life

Sometimes bad sex isn't just bad sex. Sometimes it's a crime.
There are all sorts of laws, some good, some bad, about what
kinds of sexual activities are allowed between which people.
It's tough to summarize these laws, because they can be
different depending on your age and what country and/or state
you live in. Additionally, laws about sex and sexual assault are
going through a (much-needed) period of change, so what the
law said a few years ago might not be what it says now.

The following are broad definitions of several important
legal terms related to sex, but remember: this book is meant to
provide general information and resources, and is not intended
to be a source of legal advice. If you feel you need legal advice
or representation, talk to a trusted adult about reaching out to
a licensed attorney who specializes in this area.

AGE OF CONSENT: This is the age at which you're old enough
to consent to sex. In Canada, it's age 16, while in the United
States, it's between 16 and 18, depending on the state. If you're
younger than this age, you can't legally have sex, even if you
say yes. Age-of-consent laws exist so that adults can't have sex
with minors and claim that it's okay because the minor wanted
it. Even if the minor *does* want to have sex, the law considers
them too young to be able to make that kind of decision from
an informed standpoint. There is an exception: most states
have something called "age gap laws" or "Romeo and Juliet
laws," which make sexual activity legal for minors if the people
involved are close to each other in age (two to four years apart).

STATUTORY RAPE: It may sound technical, but *statutory rape* is a generic term that is rarely used legally. It's when an adult has consensual sex with someone who is younger than the age of consent.

RAPE: Sexual intercourse (or another form of penetration by a body part or object) that someone doesn't consent to. When we think of rape, we tend to think of forcible rape, where someone uses physical force to overpower their victim, but it doesn't have to be violent to count as rape. It could be someone threatening someone else with consequences if they don't have sex, or incapacitating them with drugs or alcohol so they're less able to understand what's going on and/or to say no, or any number of other nonconsensual situations.

SEXUAL ASSAULT: A broad term that refers to any unwanted sexual touching, groping, or fondling (even through clothes) without the consent of the victim. It includes rape and attempted rape. Sexual assault is a crime.

SEXUAL COERCION: This is a specific type of sexual assault where someone coerces someone else into unwanted sexual activity by pressuring them, threatening them, or otherwise forcing them in nonphysical ways. It can involve emotional manipulation, being worn down by someone who repeatedly asks for sex despite being told no, or an authority figure using their influence to pressure someone into sex.

SEXUAL HARASSMENT: This term can mean a lot of things. Sexual harassment can be nonphysical, as when someone makes unwanted sexual comments, propositions, or threats, or it can include unwanted touching and sexual assault. It can happen at work, at school, on the street, and on social media. If it happens in the workplace, it's often illegal. If it happens at school, a law known as Title IX compels the school to protect the victim's right to an education without sexual discrimination. If you're trying to make sexual advances on someone and they're not into it, respect their boundaries and stop before you cross the line into harassment.

Types of Abuse

Abuse can come in many different forms, and it's not always easy to spot. It can look different from the abuse you may see in movies, or it can start out small before it gets bigger. One form of abuse often sets the stage for other forms, and many offenders engage in subtler forms of abuse before working their way up to physical violence or sexual assault. It is absolutely essential that your partner doesn't do any of the things in this section to you, and that you don't do any of these things to your partner.

EMOTIONAL/VERBAL ABUSE

Emotional/verbal abuse is a type of psychological abuse that uses words and nonforcible physical actions to isolate, intimidate, humiliate, or otherwise infantilize someone else. It is essentially a bullying tactic to assert the dominance of the abuser. Abuse of this type can include yelling, swearing, mocking, or even ignoring a person.

If a partner wants to know where you are and who you're with at all times, or tries to tell you who you're allowed to spend time with, that's emotional abuse. If a partner says you don't deserve love or that they're the only one who really loves you, that's emotional abuse. It is very common for the offender to deny the abuse and blame the victim. Many abusers engage in "gaslighting," claiming that events that happened are all in their victims' heads.

People being abused in this way tend to suffer from low self-esteem, depression, and anxiety. They can become withdrawn as they increasingly isolate and depend on their abusers for any sense of identity. Even if there's never any physical violence, emotional and verbal abuse still count as abuse, and they are still unacceptable.

PHYSICAL ABUSE

Physical abuse is the use of physical force against another person that results in bodily pain, injury, or impairment. It's virtually always accompanied by emotional and verbal abuse; often an abuser will start there and then escalate to physical abuse. Again, this is a behavior where the offender is trying to assert dominance and control over the victim.

Types of physical abuse might include grabbing, pinching, hair-pulling, slapping, hitting, punching, kicking, biting, burning, choking, or physically restraining someone. The abuser might use a weapon, whether that's a knife, a gun, or just a household item that they throw. Even if one instance of physical abuse seems minor or doesn't leave a mark, it's still abuse. And it's never a onetime thing—someone who physically abuses you once will do it again, and it will probably get worse over time.

Most victims of physical abuse by intimate partners are female—90 to 95 percent. Intimate-partner violence is the cause of an estimated 37 percent of injury-related emergency-room visits by women and 40 to 70 percent of all homicides involving female victims. Sadly, in the United States, intimate-partner violence seriously injures 2 million and kills 1,300 women each year.

SEXUAL ABUSE

Sexual abuse is a specific type of physical abuse where one person forces another into nonconsensual sexual activity, whether or not they use physical force. It might involve sexual assault, rape, harassment, coercion, or some combination of all these things. A sexual abuser might try to pressure their partner into unwanted sex by saying something like, "If you really loved me, you'd have sex with me" or "Sex is the only thing that would make me happy right now. Don't you want me to be happy?" If someone refuses to use a condom but insists on having sex anyway, that's sexual abuse. If someone agrees to use a condom (or other form of contraception/STI prevention) but then secretly removes that condom, that's sexual abuse.

A NOTE ABOUT BDSM

BDSM, which stands for bondage, discipline (or domination), sadism, and masochism, needs a special note here. This term refers to sexual activity that involves consensually giving and/or receiving verbal or physical domination or pain. When practiced as a form of consensual sexual play, it is not abuse, but the key word here is *consensual*. That means that both partners enthusiastically desire and explicitly verbally consent to everything that happens, and if they want to withdraw that consent at any time, they can use a safe word to stop the action and make sure everyone is okay. It's not a good idea to experiment with this kind of sexual play if you're relatively new to sex, if you sometimes find it hard to vocalize your desires or boundaries, or if one partner is into it but the other isn't.

CYBERBULLYING

The internet and social media have given us marvelous new ways to communicate and connect with each other. Unfortunately, they've also created new ways to stalk, harass, and otherwise abuse people, such as publicly posting private photos or videos of someone, or trolling someone's social media accounts with abusive comments. The anonymity of the internet means these types of abusers can often avoid getting caught. And the results can be devastating, because the bullying can reach huge numbers of people very quickly and can exist more or less permanently in cyberspace. Victims of cyberbullying, cyberstalking, and other forms of technological abuse are at risk for depression, anxiety, and even suicide.

Revenge porn is a particularly damaging form of abuse. This is when a former intimate partner publicly shares someone's private, sexually explicit photos or videos. This is never the victim's fault. Even if they consented to the photos or videos being taken at the time, they did not consent to having them shown publicly. Revenge porn moves into murky legal territory when the victim, perpetrator, or both are below the legal age of consent. Possession and distribution of child pornography is a federal crime. If you're below the age of consent and you text a sexual photo of yourself to anyone, *you* could actually be charged with distributing child pornography, whether someone uses it as revenge porn or not. The wisest thing to do is not take or send these kinds of pictures if you're under the age of consent—and if someone sends you one of these pictures, never, ever betray their trust by showing it to someone else.

Risk of serious injury or death is highest when the victim tries to leave the relationship or reports the abuse. If you have experienced anything that strikes you as abusive in this way, please seek help and get to safety as soon as possible. Consider calling the National Domestic Violence Hotline for guidance: 1-800-799-7233. If a friend has confided in you that they're being abused, let them know that you believe them, that it's not their fault, and guide them to this resource. If *you* may have acted abusively, please reach out for help. Many abusers have themselves been victims of psychological and physical abuse in their past. This is an invitation to break the cycle.

Protecting Yourself

If you have been a victim of rape, incest, or sexual assault, it is of the utmost importance to have people who support you. That means relying on your family and friends, but it also means seeking professional help to support you through your recovery. Navigating the system can be overwhelming, but you don't have to do it alone. Organizations like the Rape, Abuse & Incest National Network (RAINN) can connect you with high-quality resources and legal guidance, often for free. Call the National Sexual Assault Hotline at 1-800-656-HOPE (4673) or visit RAINN.org for help.

I was at a friend's house with a group of people and was lying down next to a guy, one of my very close friends. We had both drank a little bit, but we weren't drunk, and I started to drift in and out of sleep. I noticed his hand was going into my pants but didn't want to say anything because I was scared of confronting him. I just ignored it and pretended I was sleeping. The next day, I told some of my friends, and they confronted him. He said I made the first move by unbuttoning his pants (which wasn't true). After talking to a few more people, I found out that I wasn't the only one this had happened to. —JAZMINE, 16

Jazmine was afraid of confronting one of her very close friends. Sadly, she's not wrong to feel this way; many people react with anger to having their advances rejected. Still, it's not her fault. It was the responsibility of the guy who initiated the touch to make sure he had explicit, enthusiastic consent before he touched her. He committed sexual assault by touching her genitals without her consent, and the fact that she was pretending to be asleep makes this abundantly clear. You cannot give or receive sexual consent when you are sleeping. It sounds like this guy had a pattern of feeling entitled to access the bodies of other people without their consent. He needs to know this is unacceptable and should get help.

BAD SEX OR SEXUAL ASSAULT?

Here is the essential difference between the terms *bad sex* and *sexual assault*: bad sex is a subjective experience relating to someone's preferences, while sexual assault is the absence of a clear and enthusiastic yes.

If you and your partner have actively and mutually decided that you want to have sex, and that sex turns out to be awkward or maybe one person doesn't have an orgasm, one or both of you might consider that bad sex. But if one partner pressures or coerces the other into sex without active, affirmative, enthusiastic consent, that's sexual assault. If one partner says no five times (or even once!) but the other persists until there is simply the absence of a no (or even a weak yes), that's sexual assault. If someone says nothing at all, freezes up, and doesn't participate in sex but doesn't fight it, that's sexual assault. If one person is asleep or unconscious when sexual touch is initiated, that's sexual assault.

The difference is usually pretty clear. If it ever seems unclear to you, stop immediately and have a conversation with your partner. If you're confused or disturbed by something that may have happened in the past, reach out to a doctor, teen line, sexual assault crisis line, therapist, or trusted adult for help processing it.

IMMEDIATELY AFTER THE INCIDENT

If you contact a phone or online hotline like the ones mentioned in this book immediately after the incident, trained advocates can talk to you about what happened, connect you with local support services, and direct you to nearby health care facilities where specially trained providers can perform an exam commonly known as a "rape kit," in which they collect DNA and other evidence of sexual assault. It's essential to do this exam as close to the time of the incident as possible, even if you don't know whether you want to press charges yet. Once collected, the evidence kits can be stored for years, giving you the option of reporting and pressing charges at a later date. But if you don't have the kit and you do want to press charges, it'll be harder to prosecute your assaulter because you'll have less evidence to present.

REPORTING THE INCIDENT

There are a few ways to report a sexual assault. If you're receiving treatment for injuries or having a forensic exam, you can let a medical professional know that you want to report the crime. You can also call 911, or call or visit your local police station. Some police forces have special units with additional training and resources to handle the sensitive nature of these cases.

If the assault happened in the past, you may still be able to report it now. Statutes of limitations (the length of time after a crime during which you can still report it) vary by state. Trained advocates at an organization like RAINN can help you find out what reporting limitations apply to you and your case.

PRESSING CHARGES

Deciding whether to press charges against the person who assaulted you can be difficult.

On the one hand, most perpetrators have a pattern of behavior like this throughout their lives, and it's likely that you weren't their first victim and won't be their last. Bringing the perpetrator to justice could prevent them from violating others' human rights in the future and help send a message to all potential perpetrators that sexual violence will not be tolerated in the community.

However, the process of pressing charges can be additionally traumatizing. You might have to relive the event over and over as you describe it to law enforcement, lawyers, or a courtroom. You might have to hear a lot of strangers talking about your assault and falsely blaming you for it. And even if you go to trial, most perpetrators aren't convicted.

Only you, with the help of your support network, can decide if pressing charges is the right decision for you.

IF YOU'RE A KID

If you're a minor, especially a young kid, and you experience sexual assault, please reach out to a responsible adult and tell them what happened. If they don't help you, tell a different responsible adult. Keep telling adults about what happened until someone helps you. Sometimes adults don't have a full understanding of what constitutes sexual assault or abuse, they're in denial that something so horrible could happen, or they don't want to upset an important relationship in their own life. What happened to you was not your fault, and no matter what the person who abused or assaulted you says, you do not need to keep this kind of secret to yourself. If it feels like something that happened to you was wrong, keep telling until you get the support and understanding you need.

Similarly, if one of your friends tells you about an experience you think might be sexual abuse, you are doing the world a service by telling a responsible adult. Your friend may be too frightened or traumatized to speak up on their own behalf, but you can do it for them. You could be saving them and other victims of this perpetrator from a life of pain.

Coping with Abuse

Surviving sexual abuse of any kind can be a particularly devastating life experience. More people become seriously depressed and experience post-traumatic stress disorder (PTSD) after a sexual trauma than after any other kind of violent crime. Research suggests that survivors are 26 times more likely to abuse drugs or alcohol than people who have not experienced sexual trauma. Survivors may experience severe, debilitating anxiety, sleeplessness, and agoraphobia. The physical and psychological fallout can last a lifetime if survivors don't receive appropriate help and support to recover.

Survivors of sexual abuse are also much less likely to report the crime to law enforcement than survivors of other violent crimes, and, according to RAINN, only six of every 1,000 rapists are incarcerated (rainn.org/statistics/criminal-justice-system). Even worse, the majority of people who do report their assault say they received some kind of retaliation for it that affected their physical, social, or financial well-being.

The event itself is traumatic, but the subsequent victim blaming, shaming, self-blame, and self-doubt re-traumatize the survivor. Many of the systems in place for reporting abuse and assault can themselves involve a repeating of the trauma. This is why it's so important to get support from trained professionals to help you recover from the experience.

It's a very natural reaction to isolate yourself when you have experienced a sexual trauma. Becoming withdrawn, staying in your room, and avoiding triggers like returning to the location of the assault are all common. On college campuses (where perpetrators are almost never punished), many survivors stop going to classes or even drop out of school entirely under the strain of being forced to see their perpetrator every day. Even though this urge toward isolation is extremely common, please know that being a victim of sexual assault or abuse is never your fault, and you don't have to go through this alone.

It is not your fault someone assaulted you if you were drinking. It is not your fault if you were dressed "provocatively." It is not your fault if you were dancing. It is not your fault if you were using drugs. It is not your fault if you were dating this person or had consensual sex with them on a prior occasion. It is not your fault if you allowed them to pay for dinner or buy you drinks all evening. It is not your fault if you had been flirting or sexting with them before. It is not your fault if you didn't fight them off. It is not your fault if you froze up and went silent. It is not your fault if you didn't tell anyone immediately after the incident. It is not your fault even if you were explicitly told that it was your fault by the perpetrator, a misguided friend, a parent, a school administrator, or a health care provider. When someone violates your bodily autonomy with sexual contact without your explicit, affirmative consent, it is *simply never your fault.*

Please reach out to professionals and support groups to stay connected to community and build a support system as you move through your recovery. The National Sexual Assault Hotline (1-800-656-HOPE) can connect you quickly and confidentially to trained experts in your area. You can also access help 24/7 online by visiting rainn.org. See page 103 for even more resources.

STEP UP TO STOP SEXUAL ASSAULT

As a community, we share a collective responsibility to take care of each other as best we can. People are not perfect. They'll always make mistakes. And there will always be a few people out there who do bad things on purpose. An active, engaged community can help keep each other safe from mistakes and bad actors. Instead of abandoning people in unfortunate and traumatic circumstances, we can all step up to prevent sexual assault.

A bystander is someone who is present at but not directly taking part in a situation or event. Imagine if a bystander had intervened in all the cases of sexual harassment, coercion, or assault you've experienced or heard about. Many of these unfortunate situations could have been avoided entirely, or at least the victims could have felt supported and empowered instead of isolated and alone. You can be that active bystander and intervene when you witness bad sexual behavior. Here are some proactive tips on how to do that:

USE YOUR PRIVILEGE TO SPEAK UP FOR THOSE LESS PRIVILEGED. In the case of stopping sexual assault, it is especially powerful when men hold other men accountable for bad behavior. Often, a man is willing to listen to another man but not to a woman he's potentially about to sexually assault. Be that strong leader in a group of men who sets the standard that non-consensual sex is unacceptable behavior.

RECRUIT HELP IF YOU CAN. The more people you can bring together to step in and disrupt a bad situation, the more the perpetrator will see that their behavior is unacceptable in this community. This also keeps the perpetrator from targeting or physically threatening you. If you need to, recruit outside help like campus security or the police.

INTERRUPT THE SITUATION. The perpetrator might stop what they're doing, and their target will have a chance to get out of the situation (or, if they're unable to do it on their own, you can help them). Even interjecting with something totally unrelated, like asking for directions or pretending you're friends with the targeted person, can be helpful. The point is that the perpetrator understands that eyes are on them and that they could be held accountable for bad actions.

WATCH OUT FOR ALCOHOL. Alcohol is involved in the vast majority of sexual assaults (over 80 percent). If you see someone who is obviously quite drunk at a party, please find a friend of theirs to make sure they make it home safely. Don't leave someone passed out on a couch alone. If you see someone touching or otherwise molesting an unconscious or obviously intoxicated person, let them know you're watching and that that's sexual assault. You can even take a photo or video.

SPEAK UP ONLINE. If you witness online comments, photos, or videos that depict questionable or overtly bad sexual behavior, please call it out. If you're not sure what to say, you can use the #NotOK hashtag. When people start being challenged by peers, online or in person, they begin to act differently. It is never okay to share images of drunk people being touched inappropriately at parties. It's not funny; it's actually sexual assault.

HELP VICTIMS/SURVIVORS. Make sure they get to a safe place and receive the help and support they need. This might mean locating a friend of theirs to take them home safely, giving them the number for the National Sexual Assault Hotline (1-800-656-HOPE), or driving them to a hospital or campus health clinic and making sure they are seen by a sexual assault nurse examiner (SANE). Sometimes it means calling campus security or the police to intervene. The most important thing you can say to someone who has been through an assault is that what happened to them is not their fault, and that you will help them get whatever support they need.

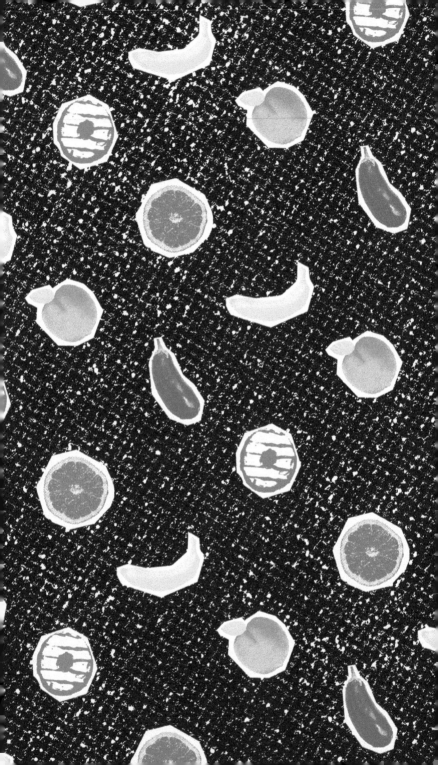

consent through your lifetime

We never get beyond the need to give and receive sexual consent. We never become entitled to unlimited access to another person's body, no matter how well we know them or how long we have been together. Nor do we ever have to put our feelings or desires aside in order to satisfy the wants or needs of our partner. This may seem like straightforward common sense, but, in fact, it is quite revolutionary. It contradicts the cultural programming so many of us receive about what rights we do and don't have over our own and others' bodies—the same programming that has led to epidemic levels of sexual assault in our society.

Our relationship with consent should start young. As a parent, I try to help my children develop a strong sense of bodily autonomy. They don't have to give anyone, adult or child, a hug or a kiss if they don't want to, and they don't get to make anyone else hug or kiss them if it's not wanted. We cannot command the physical affection of anyone, and it is important for children to know that they have a choice in the matter, that their voices will be heard, and that their bodily autonomy will be honored. As they get older, we'll start having age-appropriate conversations about sex and how, just like with hugs and kisses, no one gets to touch them if they don't want it, and they don't get to touch anyone if that person doesn't want it.

The foundational principles of empathy and mutuality discussed in this book give us a language, a sexual literacy. Fluency in this language helps us continue the process of moving with integrity and authenticity through the world. When we get in touch with ourselves and our own desires, learning to communicate with compassion and nonjudgment, we also give our partners the opportunity to connect to their own desires and find their own voice. It's a process, and no one is perfectly proficient in this language. Luckily, we have many opportunities to practice throughout our lifetime. While at first this may seem like a burden, I hope you come to see it as a precious gift.

Sexuality, with all of its nuances and forms of expression, is a wonderful part of the joy of being human. When sex involves good communication and mutual pleasure, it can lead to some of the most beautiful moments of connection and discovery that you will ever experience. I hope you have learned something in these pages, and that you'll celebrate the gift of your sexuality, free of guilt, shame, or obligation, and always with the healthy self-respect you deserve.

AFFIRMATIVE CONSENT: An explicit, informed, and voluntary agreement to participate in a sexual act.

AGE OF CONSENT: The age at which a minor can legally say yes to sexual acts. In the US, the age of consent is between 16 and 18, depending on the state.

BISEXUAL: A sexual identity used by people of all genders to indicate sexual and romantic attraction to men and women.

CAPACITY TO CONSENT: If someone is at or above the age of consent, is not overly intoxicated by drugs or alcohol, and has the physical and intellectual ability to freely give affirmative consent for a sexual interaction, they have the capacity to consent.

CISGENDER: Relating to a person whose inner sense of personal identity and gender corresponds to the sex they were assigned at birth. Often abbreviated as "cis."

CONTRACEPTION: Something used during sex to prevent pregnancy. The most common contraceptives are condoms (barrier method) and birth control pills (hormonal method).

EMOTIONAL/VERBAL ABUSE: A type of psychological abuse that uses words and nonforcible physical actions to isolate, intimidate, and humiliate someone else.

GAY: A sexual identity primarily used by men to indicate sexual and romantic attraction to other men.

HETEROSEXUAL/STRAIGHT: A sexual identity primarily used by men to indicate their sexual and romantic attraction to women or by women to indicate their sexual and romantic attraction to men.

INCAPACITATION RAPE: Nonconsensual sex (forcible or not) when someone is so intoxicated that they no longer have the ability to give explicit affirmative consent.

LESBIAN: A sexual identity primarily used by women to indicate sexual and romantic attraction to other women.

PANSEXUAL: A sexual identity used by people of all genders to indicate sexual and romantic attraction to people of any gender.

PHYSICAL ABUSE: The intentional use of physical force against another person that results in bodily pain, injury, or impairment.

QUEER: Sometimes used as an umbrella term for non-heterosexual and non-normative sexualities and genders; a more fluid, non-binary, and often more explicitly political identity as compared to gay, lesbian, or bisexual.

RAPE: Sexual intercourse (or other form of penetration by a body part or object) without the consent of the victim. This can include forcible rape, incapacitation rape, or any number of other nonconsensual situations.

SEXTING: Sending photos, videos, or texts of a sexual nature through social media or other messaging apps.

SEXUAL ASSAULT: A broad term for sexual activity without the consent of the victim, which includes unwanted sexual touching, groping or fondling, attempted rape, and rape.

SEXUAL COERCION: Sexual assault that the perpetrator achieves by pressuring, threatening, tricking, or otherwise forcing someone to have sex without using physical force.

SEXUAL HARASSMENT: Bullying or harassment of a sexual nature, including sexual coercion. In the workplace, sexual harassment that leads to a hostile work environment or results in a negative employment decision (such as quitting, demoting, or firing) is illegal.

SEXUALLY TRANSMITTED INFECTIONS (STIS): Infections, viral or bacterial, that are transmitted by sexual contact. They have previously been called "venereal diseases" or STDs.

STATUTORY RAPE: Nonforcible sexual activity between an adult and a minor, when the minor is past the age of puberty but below the age of consent.

STEALTHING: The intentional removal of a condom by one partner without the consent of the other partner. It is a form of sexual assault.

TITLE IX: One part of the Education Amendments of 1972, a comprehensive federal civil rights law that prohibits discrimination on the basis of sex in educational institutions or programs that receive federal funding. In the 1990s, three US Supreme Court decisions ruled that this protection against discrimination applies to cases of sexual harassment, coercion, and assault.

TRANSGENDER: Relating to a person whose gender does not correspond with the sex they were assigned at birth.

BOOKS

S.E.X.: The All-You-Need-To-Know Sexuality Guide to Get You Through Your Teens and Twenties, second edition, by Heather Corinna (Da Capo Lifelong Books, 2016).

A comprehensive, up-to-date text with inclusive information on all sexuality-related topics for teens and young adults.

Make Love Not Porn: Technology's Hardcore Impact on Human Behavior by Cindy Gallop (TED Books, 2011).

A call to action for society to acknowledge how hardcore pornography is shaping and distorting the ways today's young men and women think about sex and intimacy. An impassioned plea for a new kind of porn that reflects a more realistic version of human sexuality, with respect, dignity, equity, and mutuality.

She Comes First: The Thinking Man's Guide to Pleasuring a Woman by Ian Kerner (William Morrow, 2009).

A must-read for all young men (and women) who have sex with women, emphasizing the female sexual response cycle and the importance of mutual pleasure for healthy and gratifying sexual experiences.

The Consent Guidebook: A Practical Approach to Consensual, Respectful, and Enthusiastic Interactions by Erin Tillman (AuthorHouse, 2018).

A clear, concise, and inclusive guidebook that lays out essential definitions and provides an excellent tool kit for healthy and consensual sexual interactions.

ONLINE & TELEPHONE RESOURCES

RAINN/NATIONAL SEXUAL ASSAULT HOTLINE: The nation's largest organization that works to prevent and deal with the aftermath of sexual violence. Call 1-800-656-HOPE (4673) or visit RAINN.org.

SCARLETEEN: Inclusive, comprehensive, supportive information about sexuality and relationships for teenagers and young adults. Visit Scarleteen.com.

NATIONAL DOMESTIC VIOLENCE HOTLINE: A 24-hour confidential service available to help victims and survivors of domestic violence. Trained counselors can be reached by phone or online chat. Call 1-800-799-SAFE (7233) or visit TheHotline.org.

END RAPE ON CAMPUS (EROC): A survivor-advocacy organization dedicated to ending sexual violence through survivor support, public education, and policy reform at the campus, local, state, and federal levels. Visit EndRapeOnCampus.org.

CRISIS TEXT LINE: A free, 24/7, confidential text-message service for people in crisis. Visit CrisisTextLine.org or text HOME to 741741 in the United States.

TEEN LINE: If you have a problem or just want to talk with another teen who understands, then this is the right place for you! Teens helping teens for 34 years. Call 310-855-4673, text TEEN to 839863, or visit TeenLineOnline.org.

A CALL TO MEN: Help create a world where all men and boys are loving and respectful, and all women and girls are valued and safe. Visit ACallToMen.org.

Child Trends. "Dating." ChildTrends.org. Updated December 2015. https://www.childtrends.org/indicators/dating.

Dube, Shanta R., Robert F. Anda, Charles L. Whitfield, David W. Brown, Vincent J. Felitti, Maxia Dong, and Wayne H. Giles. "Long-Term Consequences of Childhood Sexual Abuse by Gender of Victim." *American Journal of Preventive Medicine* 28, no. 5 (June 2005): 430–438. doi:10.1016/j.amepre.2005.01.015.

Finer, Lawrence B. "Trends in Premarital Sex in the United States, 1954–2003." *Public Health Reports* 122, no. 1 (January–February 2007): 73–78. doi:10.1177/003335490712200110.

Finer, L. B., and J. M. Philbin. "Trends in Ages at Key Reproductive Transitions in the United States, 1951–2010." *Women's Health Issues* 24, no. 3 (2014): e271–e279. doi:10.1016/j.whi.2014.02.002.

Francoeur, Robert T., and Raymond J. Noonan, eds. *The Continuum Complete International Encyclopedia of Sexuality*. New York: The Continuum International Publishing Group, Inc., 2004.

Guttmacher Institute. "Adolescent Sexual and Reproductive Health in the United States." Guttmacher.org. Accessed August 3, 2018. https://www.guttmacher.org/fact-sheet/american-teens-sexual -and-reproductive-health.

———. "Sex and HIV Education." Guttmacher.org. Accessed August 3, 2018. https://www.guttmacher.org/state-policy/explore /sex-and-hiv-education.

Hazan, Cindy and Phillip Shaver. "Romantic Love Conceptualized as an Attachment Process." *Journal of Personality and Social Psychology* 52, no. 3 (March 1987): 511–524. doi:10.1037/0022 -3514.52.3.511.

Kann, Laura, Tim McManus, William A. Harris, Shari L. Shanklin, Katherine H. Flint, Joseph Hawkins, Barbara Queen, et al. "Youth Risk Behavior Surveillance—United States, 2015." *Morbidity and Mortality Weekly Report Surveillance Summaries* 65, no. 6 (June 10, 2016). https://www.cdc.gov/healthyyouth/data/yrbs/pdf/2015 /ss6506_updated.pdf.

Kann, Laura, Emily O'Malley Olsen, Tim McManus, William A. Harris, Shari L. Shanklin, Katherine H. Flint, Barbara Queen, et al. "Sexual Identity, Sex of Sexual Contacts, and Health-Related Behaviors Among Students in Grades 9–12—United States and Selected Sites, 2015." *Morbidity and Mortality Weekly Report Surveillance Summaries* 65, no. 9 (August 12, 2016). https://www.cdc .gov/mmwr/volumes/65/ss/pdfs/ss6509.pdf.

Kilpatrick, Dean G. "The Mental Health Impact of Rape." National Violence Against Women Prevention Research Center, Medical University of South Carolina (2000). Accessed August 27, 2018. https://mainweb-v.musc.edu/vawprevention/research /mentalimpact.shtml.

Martinez, Gladys M., and Joyce C. Abma. "Sexual Activity, Contraceptive Use, and Childbearing of Teenagers Aged 15–19 in the United States." *NCHS Data Brief* no. 209 (2015). https://www.cdc .gov/nchs/products/databriefs/db209.htm.

Masters, William H., and Virginia E. Johnson. *Human Sexual Response*. New York: Bantam, 1981. 1st ed. 1966.

McQuillan, Geraldine, Deanna Kruszon-Moran, Elaine W. Flagg, and Ryne Paulose-Ram. "Prevalence of Herpes Simplex Virus Type 1 and Type 2 in Persons Aged 14–49: United States, 2015–2016."

NCHS Data Brief no. 304 (February 2018). https://www.cdc.gov
/nchs/data/databriefs/db304.pdf.

Mehrabian, Albert. *Silent Messages: Implicit Communication of Emotions and Attitudes*. 2nd ed. Belmont, CA: Wadsworth Publishing Company, 1981.

National Conference of State Legislatures. "State Policies on Sex Education in Schools." NCSL.org. December 21, 2016. http://www
.ncsl.org/research/health/state-policies-on-sex-education-in
-schools.aspx.

Planned Parenthood. "Birth Control." PlannedParenthood.org. Accessed August 3, 2018. https://www.plannedparenthood.org
/learn/birth-control.

Rape, Abuse & Incest National Network (RAINN). "The Criminal Justice System: Statistics." Accessed August 27, 2018. https://rainn
.org/statistics/criminal-justice-system.

Sabina, Chiara, Janis Wolak, and David Finkelhor. "The Nature and Dynamics of Internet Pornography Exposure for Youth." *CyberPsychology & Behavior* 11, no. 6 (December 11, 2008): 691–3. doi:10.1089/cpb.2007.0179.

Santelli, John S., Leslie M. Kantor, Stephanie A. Grilo, Ilene S. Speizer, Laura D. Lindberg, Jennifer Heitel, Amy T. Schalet, et al. "Abstinence-Only-Until-Marriage: An Updated Review of U.S. Policies and Programs and Their Impact." *Journal of Adolescent Health* 61, no. 3 (September 2017): 273–280. doi:10.1016
/j.jadohealth.2017.05.031.

Stanger-Hall, Kathrin F., and David W. Hall. "Abstinence-Only Education and Teen Pregnancy Rates: Why We Need Comprehensive Sex Education in the U.S." *PLoS ONE* 6, no. 10 (2011): e24658. doi:10.1371/journal.pone.0024658.

U.S. Department of Health and Human Services, Office of Adolescent Health and Administration on Children, Youth, and Families. "Teens in the United States: Trends in Behavior and Attitudes Related to Pregnancy and Childbearing." HHS.gov. https://www .hhs.gov/ash/oah/sites/default/files/teensexualbehavior.pdf.

Wylie, K. R., and I. Eardley. "Penile Size and the 'Small Penis Syndrome.'" *BJU International* 99, no. 6 (June 2007): 1449–55. doi:10.1111/j.1464-410X.2007.06806.x.

Xu, Fujie, Julia A. Schillinger, Maya R. Sternberg, Robert E. Johnson, Francis K. Lee, Andre J. Nahmias, and Lauri E. Markowitz. "Seroprevalence and Coinfection with Herpes Simplex Virus Type 1 and Type 2 in the United States, 1988–1994." *The Journal of Infectious Diseases* 185, no. 8 (April 15, 2002): 1019–1024. doi:10.1086/340041.

Xu, Fujie, Maya R. Sternberg, and Benny J. Kottiri. "Trends in Herpes Simplex Virus Type 1 and Type 2 Seroprevalence in the United States." *Journal of the American Medical Association* 296, no. 8 (August 23/30, 2006): 964–973. doi:10.1001/jama.296.8.964.

INDEX

ACKNOWLEDGMENTS

I have to begin by thanking all of the feminist educators, activists, and policy makers through the generations. Your courage, hard work, and perseverance continue to make the world a safer, healthier place for people of all genders.

To the professionals who work in the fields of sex-positivity, sexual somatic healing, clinical psychotherapy, and survivor and crisis support services, who have somehow inspired and supported the content of this book—especially Nancy Lublin, Gabriella Cordova, Dr. Laurie Bennett-Cook, Rahi Chun, Dr. Lauren Brim, Pamela Wylie-Samuelson, and Dr. Tim Beyer— thank you. Your love, compassion, and ability to hold space for powerful healing in this world take my breath away.

Molly Abrams, Max Moore, and all members of the "OG" and "Pali-High" Lit Clubs who inspired the original idea for this book: Thank you for explaining the need to have quality sex ed resources in the curriculum of schools and in the hands of teens and young adults *before* they need it. Thank you to Izzy Moore, my teen editorial board, and to all the young people who anonymously shared their experiences for this book.

Lauren Abrams, Jenn Duncan, Shaneen Gottula, Elena Christopoulos, Amy Ziering, and all my amazing women who have encouraged, critiqued, and otherwise birthed this title into being: I love you and am so deeply grateful that you are in my life.

To survivors, and to every voice that has ever said #MeToo—thank you for your courage. By sharing our stories, we let others know that they are not alone. We have changed the national conversation on the issue of consent and sex, and future generations will face less shame and stigma and find more support because of us.

Deep gratitude goes out to Rob Kramer, my friend and business partner at Buzz Labs, and the brilliant and creative team at New Deal Design, who believed in our vision of empowering young adults with technology that brings people together to create healthier communities around sex and dating.

Finally, to Peter, my life partner and the most important teacher on this subject I have ever had: Thank you for your love and your patience.

JENNIFER LANG, MD, is the cofounder and creator of Buzz Labs, a social impact tech start-up innovating products for the movement to end sexual violence. She received her medical education at Albert Einstein College of Medicine in New York, where she received the Dean's Award: "Holding Promise for the Future of Medicine." She completed her residency in Obstetrics and Gynecology at St. Luke's/Roosevelt Hospital Center of Columbia University College of Physicians and Surgeons, then a fellowship in Gynecologic Oncology at UCLA and Cedars-Sinai Medical Centers. She practiced as a board-certified ob-gyn and gynecologic oncologist, specializing in integrative and preventative medicine, and minimally invasive and robotic surgery. In 2013, she cofounded an international medical nonprofit that delivers cervical cancer prevention services to women in resource-poor countries. Since then, the nonprofit has grown to support 80 clinics spanning Africa, Asia, the Caribbean, and Central America. She is the author of *The Whole 9 Months: A Week-By-Week Pregnancy Nutrition Guide with Recipes for a Healthy Start* (Sonoma Press, 2016), and mother of three intelligent (and slightly precocious) kids, who always ask the hardest questions.